MIXED BLESSINGS

by

Barbara Brown Taylor

SUSAN HUNTER

Publishing

Atlanta, Georgia

Published by Susan Hunter Publishing, Atlanta, Georgia
Manufactured in the United States of America
5 4 3 2 1

Publisher: Susan Hunter
Editor: Phyllis Mueller
Illustrations: Judy Barber
Back Cover Photo: Lynda Greer

Library of Congress Cataloging-in-Publication Data

Taylor, Barbara Brown.
Mixed blessings.

Includes index.
1. Sermons, American. I. Title
BV4253.T39 1986   252   86-20975
ISBN 0-932419-05-4

TABLE OF CONTENTS

I. THE CLOUD OF WITNESSES

II. THE FIRSTBORN OF ALL CREATION

III. THE INHABITANTS OF EARTH

for Edward

So Jacob was left alone, and a man wrestled with him there till daybreak. When the man saw that he could not throw Jacob, he struck him in the hollow of his thigh, so that Jacob's hip was dislocated as they wrestled. The man said, "Let me go, for day is breaking," but Jacob replied, "I will not let you go unless you bless me."

Genesis 32.24–26 NEB

INTRODUCTION

There are a number of good reasons why a preacher might worry about seeing her sermons in print. In the first place, a printed sermon is something of a contradiction in terms. A sermon is, by definition, a form of speech – a conversation between a preacher and a congregation at a particular time in their lives together, informed by their common worship and reading of scripture. It is a fluid word that is spoken, fluid and warm and transient. Between the covers of a book that same word becomes fixed; it cools off, and takes on a different sound.

Then there is the matter of acknowledgements. Preaching is at best a communal art, each sermon a pieced quilt of shared stories and borrowed phrases, remembered but rarely documented. There are no footnotes from the pulpit, and trying to reconstruct them after the fact is like trying to recall where all the pieces of the quilt came from: there are so many pieces, so many people to thank for them, but most of the connections are gone. What remains is a quilt, or a sermon, stitched together with material from many lives. It does not belong to any one person, but to everyone who participates in it.

Lastly, there is the issue of repetition. The danger of collecting seventeen sermons together in one place is that they may turn out to be one sermon in seventeen different disguises. That is certainly the case with these sermons. Over and over, their one refrain is that life is full of blessings – mixed blessings, perhaps, but blessings nonetheless – and that the job of the believer is to root those blessings out: to search for them, to insist on them, to wrestle angels for them if necessary, refusing to let go until we have blessings to show for our wounds. We may limp for the rest of our lives, but what our lame gait proclaims by faith is that we have been blessed.

It is the wish for that one refrain to be heard that allows a preacher to overcome her several worries and pack her sermons off to the printer. These particular sermons are all lectionary sermons, prepared in light of the weekly readings assigned by *The Book of Common Prayer*. As such, they often hunt the relationship between seemingly unrelated passages of scripture, a discipline guaranteed to keep the most energetic Bible students on their toes. For those who are interested, there is a scriptural index at the back of the book that lists the three readings for each sermon.

While it may not be possible properly to attribute each sermon, there are a number of people to thank for the material that makes up this patchwork collection. Frederick Buechner, for one, whose influence here will be apparent to anyone familiar with his work; and Harry Pritchett, for another, to whom I am indebted for far more than his story in the last sermon of this book. I am also grateful to the men and women of the Thursday Bible Class, whose struggles with the weekly lections have blessed me richly, and to Sue Oldham, the friend who talks to trees. Finally, my thanks to Susan Hunter, whose idea this was, to Judy Barber, whose drawings speak volumes, to Bill, Phyllis, Roy, Brad, Grace, Earl and the gracious people of All Saints' Episcopal Church, to whom these sermons belong.

Barbara Brown Taylor
Atlanta, Georgia

I.
THE CLOUD
OF
WITNESSES

ABRAM
Wed By God

Abram believed in the Lord, and he reckoned it to him as righteousness. And he said to him, "I am the Lord who brought you from Ur of the Chaldeans, to give you this land to possess." But he said, "O Lord God, how am I to know that I shall possess it?" He said to him, "Bring me a heifer three years old, a she-goat three years old, a ram three years old, a turtledove, and a young pigeon." And he brought him all these, cut them in two, and laid each half over against the other; but he did not cut the birds in two. And when the birds of prey came down upon the carcasses, Abram drove them away. As the sun was going down, a deep sleep fell on Abram; and lo, a dread and great darkness fell upon him. When the sun had gone down and it was dark, behold, a smoking fire pot and a flaming torch passed between these pieces. On that day the Lord made a covenant with Abram . . .
Genesis 15.6-12, 17-18 RSV

Someone asked him, 'Sir, are only a few to be saved?' His answer was: 'Struggle to get in through the narrow door; for I tell you that many will try to enter and not be able. When once the master of the house has got up and locked the door, you may stand outside and knock, and say, "Sir, let us in!" but he will only answer, "I do not know where you come from."

Luke 13.23-24 NEB

Here is a Sunday full of contradictions. It is a Sunday when we are invited to contemplate our failures, but also one in which we are reminded who we are and where we belong. We are the workers of iniquity, killers of the prophets and enemies of the cross of Christ. But we are also the heirs of Abraham, citizens of the commonwealth of heaven, and members of Christ's glorious body. Identity crisis, anyone? Do we sing alleluias or run for cover, praise God or beg his eternal pardon?

Let us begin at the beginning, about 4000 years ago, with the story of God's covenant with our forefather Abram. His name is still Abram, by the way – it is not until a couple of chapters later in Genesis that God changes his name to Abraham, meaning "father of a multitude." In today's story he is just plain old Abram, an elderly Jew without an heir who believes God's promise of a son and a land but would prefer proof. "O Lord God," he asks, "how am I to know that I shall possess it?" So proof is what he gets, a covenant with God that takes place in the middle of the night among a whole barnyard of slaughtered animals. It is a rather bizarre scene to our modern eyes, but it was an accepted way of sealing a covenant in Abram's day: take a bunch of good-sized animals, halve them as neatly as you can, clear a path between the pieces and require each partner to walk between them as a sort of self-curse. By passing through the severed bodies of the animals each partner says, in effect, "May the same thing happen to me if I do not keep my word." It is what we promise but never mean when we say, "Cross my heart and hope to die, stick a needle in my eye."

So that is how Abram got himself in partnership with God, and it is a scene that shows us our age. While we serenely approach an altar stained only with candle wax, Abram waded blood to get to his, waving his arms at the vultures who made off with an eye or a bit of fur before he could drive the big birds away. Then night fell and he was dozing on his feet, worn out with the effort of rounding up and butchering the stubborn animals. He slept, but fitfully, that awful kind of sleep in which you tell yourself the gorilla standing over your bed is not real but you cannot be sure, that kind of sleep in which something infinitely dark and heavy seats itself on your chest and takes your breath away. In the midst of such a sleep Abram saw a pot of fire, a flaming torch, pass between the halves of the slain animals. It was the Lord, keeping his end of the bargain, the Lord who spoke, repeating his promise of descendents for Abram, and of a land for them all to live in.

This haunting story, so far from our own experience, is nonetheless the story of our own beginnings with God as his chosen people, and it is full of real things: blood and guts, faith and doubt, fear and promise. Above all it is full of real relationship: God and Abram talk to one another; God tells Abram what to do and he does it; Abram keeps his part of the covenant and God comes through with his. In short, Abram is chosen and he knows it. So what happened? By the time we get to the story from Luke some 2000 years later, God's chosen people are well on their way to becoming God's frozen people, standing in the street listening to the sounds of a banquet from which they have been excluded. Many will stand at the narrow door and knock, we are told, but the voice inside will deny any relationship at all. "I do not know where you come from," the Lord will say, "I do not know you at all."

Here is the worst judgment of all, not being sentenced to roast in hell but being left out of heaven, separated for all time from the place we most want to be and the people we most want to be with, and all because we would not, in our lifetimes, be with the people God sent us, prophets and messengers who told us things about ourselves we did not want to hear. We thought we were fine; they told us were sick unto death. We thought we were rich; they told us we were poor in the things that mattered. We thought we could take care of ourselves; they told us we were in desperate need of a savior, someone to thaw our hardened hearts and lead us home.

"O Jerusalem, Jerusalem, killing the prophets and stoning those who are sent to you! How often would I have gathered your children together as a hen gathers her brood under her wings, and you would not! Behold, your house is forsaken. And I tell you, you will not see me until you say, 'Blessed is he who comes in the name of the Lord!'" Well. Is the verdict in, then? Has the final sentence been pronounced? Are we in or out? Acquitted or condemned? Is the door still open or has the banquet begun without us? Dear God, it is a frightening thing to come under your judgment. And you, Jesus, the one we thought we could count on for sympathy and understanding, is that really you closing the door in our faces? Don't you care about us anymore?

On the slopes of the Mount of Olives, some distance from Jerusalem, there stands even today a small chapel called *Dominus Fleuvit,* a Latin name that means "the Lord wept." According to legend it marks the spot where today's story from Luke took place, where Jesus stood looking across the Kedron Valley at the great city of Jerusalem and pronounced judgment on it. At least that is one way of looking at what he did. Remembering how many prophets had been put to death there and guessing – correctly – that he would be next, he either pronounced judgment on Jerusalem or lamented the loss of her love, or both, but in any case he wept, and his words are familiar to any of us who have ever loved someone who would not love us back. *Have it your way. I would have loved you like no one ever did; I would have taken care of you. But I get the message; you don't want my love. Well to hell with you and what you want. You won't see me any more, but mark my words – you'll miss me when I am gone. You'll be sorry you threw my love away.* And *dominus fleuvit;* the Lord wept.

Here is a whisper of the Good News, if we can hear it over the sound of a breaking heart. This is no impassive judge rendering his verdict from on high; this is someone in love with us, whose dire threats reveal not his despisal of us but his incredible devotion to us. Hell hath no fury like a Messiah scorned – "And I tell you, you will not see me," he says – but even in the midst of his pain and grief this lover who is also our Lord cracks the narrow door for us. "You will not see me until you say, 'Blessed is he who comes in the name of the Lord,'" he says, letting us know that nothing – not our rejection of him, not our failure to follow him, not even our hanging him on a cross – can separate us from the everlasting offer of his love. If ever we can find it in our hearts to bless him, to love him, and live as if we do, he will rush out to meet us and bring us home.

But you do not have to believe all this. It may not even matter to you whether we are judged by an impartial counselor at law or a long lost lover who wants us back, but if you choose the lover then even the Abram story takes on a different cast. The covenant between the old man and his God becomes a wedding covenant, only Abram has no choice. God does not say, "Will you marry me?" He says, "You are mine," and Abram's only choice is whether to believe it, whether to act like it is true, or not. According to the record he did not even want time to think about it. He believed, presumably because the world made no sense if he did not, and he became God's partner in a covenant that changed the face of history.

As Abram's heirs we too are wed to a God we did not choose but who chose us, a God who – with the birth of a son – became bone of our bone and flesh of our flesh. It may have been Abram who passed through the pieces that haunted night long ago, but the covenant survives as our own. What God has joined together let no one put asunder, and let those who try make no mistake: when we attempt to cut God out of our lives we bleed, and that is not wishful thinking but the soul's own truth.

So it is, perhaps, not guilt that we are invited to feel today but love. It is a love with consequences, but it is also a love that never ends, and that depends less on our behavior than on our understanding of who – and whose – we are. The hen does not want to gather us under her great sheltering wings because we are good but because we are *hers*. It is a love story we are in, but like so many love story characters we do not understand that until the one who loves us dies. Sure, if we had been there we would have dried his tears and blessed his name a thousand times, but we were not, and he is gone, at least the part of him we might have touched. So what do we do now?

Remember the covenant. Love him by loving one another. Love him in his absence by loving his presence in each other as he himself has loved us: not as a cool, impartial judge but as a lover who never tires of forgiveness, who waits just behind the door we have failed to show up at and – at the first tap from us, the first sign of our changed hearts – opens it wide to embrace us and take us home.

MOSES
Uncommon Light

Moses was minding the flock of his father-in-law Jethro, priest of Midian. He led the flock along the side of the wilderness and came to Horeb, the mountain of God. There the angel of the Lord appeared to him in the flame of a burning bush. Moses noticed that, although the bush was on fire, it was not being burnt up; so he said to himself, "I must go across to see this wonderful sight. Why does not the bush burn away?" When the Lord saw that Moses had turned aside to look, he called to him out of the bush, "Moses, Moses." And Moses answered, "Yes, I am here." God said, "Come no nearer; take off your sandals; the place where you are standing is holy ground." Then he said, "I am the God of your forefathers, the God of Abraham, the God of Isaac, the God of Jacob." Moses covered his face, for he was afraid to gaze on God.

Exodus 3.1-6 NEB

Let me begin by confessing a certain amount of hypocrisy in what I am about to say. While I exhort other people to slow down and look inward, to discern the movement of God in their lives, I myself continue to dash around, running errands, responding to real or imagined needs, minding all the sheep of my life, if you will, all the while ignoring the voice that calls to me to stop, just *stop* a minute and wait on the Lord. So I was not going to write a new sermon for this occasion. I was going to choose a respectable effort from the past and spruce it up a little, thereby leaving myself more time to rent vans for the parish retreat this weekend, to order food for the confirmation class dinner next week. You get the picture. Then I ran across this passage from Exodus, the story about Moses and the burning bush, and my week was shot. The story was for me, and for you, and for all of us who are afflicted with busy-ness – the story of a man who turned aside from what he was doing to encounter the living God.

At the beginning of the story, you will remember, Moses is a fugitive from justice. He has killed a man in Egypt and fled some 200 miles across the Sinai peninsula to the land of Midian, where he has married a Midianite woman and plans, presumably, to hide himself for the rest of his life. It is a comfortable exile, however; he has everything he wants, including a son, and his father-in-law Jethro is a well-to-do priest with plenty of land and livestock. So Moses goes to work for him, and gradually his bad memories of Egypt fade. Then one day he is minding Jethro's flock in the desert country around Mount Horeb, minding his own business, when he sees a bush out in the middle of nowhere, burning for all it is worth. He considers the possibilities: a bolt of wayward lightning? Spontaneous combustion? Perhaps one of the sheep's hooves stuck a flint. Or maybe it only looks like it is burning; it could be some kind of phosphorescence, or a fake rigged up with foil and red lights, some Midianite's idea of a joke. But no, he can smell it, aromatic as incense, and he can see the column of heat rising into the air above the bush. The odd thing is that it does not quit; as long as Moses stands there watching it he never sees a single twig turn to ash. Glowing like a coal beneath the flames the bush is not diminished, and finally Moses has to take a closer look. "I must go across and see this wonderful sight," he says. "Why does not the bush burn away?"

When the Lord sees that Moses has turned aside to look, that he has let the sheep wander in order to pay attention to the miracle right under his nose, then and only then does the Lord speak to him out of the bush, calling him by name and telling him to take off his shoes. Which Moses is reluctant to do, incidentally, standing so near that popping ball of fire. But he does, and as he listens the Lord identifies himself. He is not one of the local, lesser gods; he is the God of Abraham, Isaac and Jacob, the God of Moses' ancestors. He identifies himself by his relationship to those people, and his history with them. He has heard them crying, he tells Moses, he has seen how badly they have been treated in Egypt and he wants Moses to arrange their escape.

Now this sounds like a very bad idea to Moses. In the first place, he is a wanted man. If he goes back to Egypt he might as well walk straight into police headquarters and give himself up. And in the second place, he has some major misgivings about his leadership ability. "Who am I that I should bring the Israelites out of Egypt?" he asks the bush, and it is no false humility on his part. He can barely lead sheep; what will he do with an entire nation? God does not offer much reassurance, at least not the kind Moses wants, like a guarantee of safe passage and a game plan. He does not say, "Nothing bad will happen to you." He says, "I am with you," as if that were enough. "Never mind who you are," he says, in effect, "what matters is who I am and that I have chosen you."

Looking for any leverage he can find, Moses decides to try and find out exactly whom this bush and this voice belong to. Sure, they belong to the God of Abraham, Isaac and Jacob, but what is this God's own name? What is his essence? If Moses can discover that, he may have a little power over this deity who is asking so much of him. But he is too clever to ask directly. "If I go to the Israelites and tell them the god of their forefathers has sent me and they ask me his name, what shall I say?" he inquires of the bush. Not that I want to know for myself, you understand, but if they should ask, who shall I say is calling? "I am who I am," God answers. "Tell them that 'I am' has sent you." Now what kind of answer is that? Imagine sitting next to someone at a dinner party. You introduce yourself and talk a little while before you realize you never caught the other person's name. "Excuse me," you say politely, "but what was your name?"

"I am who I am," the person says. "I was who I was, I am who I am, I will be who I will be." In other words, it is none of your business who I am. If we are afraid to call it an impudent answer, it is at least an evasive one. By giving us such a puzzling name God lets us know that there is no controlling him. "I will be gracious unto whom I will be gracious," he says later in Exodus, "and I will have compassion on whom I will have compassion. Furthermore, my face you cannot see, for no mortal man may see me and live." It is an answer, at any rate, that puts Moses in his place. He decides to believe his burning bush, he accepts his call, and he never sees more than the backside of God again, but even that is catching; after many such encounters with the God of the burning bush his own face begins to shine, to burn with such bright light that he frightens those around him and takes to wearing a veil. The end of the story, of course, is that he delivers Israel to the promised land and becomes one of the heros of the faith.

Those were the good old days: burning bushes, angels of the Lord, pillars of fire, parted seas – all those unmistakable signs of the presence of God. What wouldn't we give for one clear direction from the Lord, one burning bush to call us by name and tell us what to do? At least I think that is what I want. I stay so busy sometimes I wonder if I would see it; I wonder if I am so focused on my list of things to do that I would not notice a burning bush until I was scorched by it. And then, like Moses, I am afraid, afraid of what the bush might know about me, afraid of what it might ask me to do. If I stay busy with the little things, maybe God will not notice me; maybe he will see that I already have enough to do and call on someone else to do the big things. So I just hunch my shoulders, keep my head down, and mind my own business. A burning bush? I didn't see it. A burning bush? I haven't got time. A burning bush? There is a reasonable explanation. A burning bush? Someone, please, put it out.

I have a friend who is not as busy as I am. She takes lots of walks, and while she has never claimed to see a burning bush, she does admit to talking somewhat frequently with trees. Once, she says, she was walking along fretting about how she ought to be, things she ought to change about herself, when this big poplar said, "Hey, why do you worry so much? Watch me be a tree." So she just stood there a minute or two and watched the tree be a perfectly acceptable tree. "Okay," the tree said, "Now you go be you." And she did.

Then there was the time she was mulling over everything that had gone wrong lately and ran into a maple with great upswept branches. "Try it," the tree said, and she did, lifting up her arms and looking into the deep blue of the sky. All of a sudden, she said, she understood that it was a gesture of thankfulness, and with that understanding she herself became full of gratitude. "Thanks," she said to the tree. "Don't mention it," the tree replied.

It is not just trees that talk to her. Once it was a stunning sunset that said, "Do not worry too much about the world. I can handle it," and once it was some river rapids that said, "I know it looks rough to you right now, but there is a real quiet stretch a little further along. Trust me." Trust me. Trust the poplar, the maple, the sunset, the river. Trust God to inhabit every living thing and use it to announce his presence. Trust yourself enough to notice and turn aside.

My friend reminds me of Gerard Manley Hopkins, a poet and Roman Catholic priest who lived and wrote during the last half of the nineteenth century. He felt torn between his love of God and his love of writing, and more than once he burned his poetry, resolving to write no more. Still, he kept a journal of notes – about the state of his own soul but also about everything he saw in the world. "For Lent," he wrote in 1866, "No puddings on Sundays. No tea except if to keep me awake and then without sugar. Meat only once a day. No verses in passion week or on Fridays. No lunch or meat on Fridays. Not to sit in armchair except can work in no other way. Ash Wednesday and Good Friday bread and water."

Thus the priest tried to limit his appetite for the world, but the burning bushes would not stop; the poet saw everything: "Drops of rain hanging on rails," his next entry reads, "seen only with the lower rim lighted like nails (of fingers) . . . mealy clouds with a not brilliant moon. Blunt buds of the ash. Pencil buds of the beech. Lobes of the trees. Cups of the eyes. Gathering back the lightly hinged eyelids. Bows of the eyelids. Pencil of eyelashes. Juices of the eyeball. Eyelids like leaves, petals, caps, tufted hats, handkerchiefs, sleeves, gloves. Also of the bones sleeved in flesh. Juices of the sunrise."

The man saw everything, and in everything he saw God. "The world is charged with the grandeur of God," he wrote at last. "It will flame out, like shining from shook foil." That is something the poets among us have always known. "Earth's crammed with heaven," wrote Hopkins' contemporary Elizabeth Barrett Browning, "each common bush aflame with God. Yet only he who sees takes off his shoes. The rest set round and pluck blackberries." Or tend sheep. Or run errands. Fill in your own blank. Then stop, if you are willing. Stop and take off your shoes, knowing that wherever you are is holy ground. Risk getting burned, looking foolish, being wrong. Drop what you are doing and turn aside, to look into every bush, every face, every event of your life – the big and the small, the hoped for and the feared, the bad and the good – look into every one of them for God's presence and call. Believe that, whatever is going on, God is in it, and can be trusted.

Finally, if you are still willing, go the last step. Once you have gotten the knack of seeing burning bushes everywhere, consent to be set on fire yourself, to be for someone else the presence and call of God. Like Moses without his veil, go ahead and frighten people with your shining face, so full of uncommon light, so alive with unimagined possibility that sometimes the fire scares even you. It may or may not hurt, but we will not be consumed, and we will not be alone. "I am who I am" is with us, and has been with us all along, and will be with us forever, world without end.

SAMUEL
Voices in the Night

Now Samuel did not yet know the Lord, and the word of the Lord had not yet been revealed to him. And the Lord called Samuel again the third time. And he arose and went to Eli, and said, "Here I am, for you called me." Then Eli perceived that the Lord was calling the boy. Therefore Eli said to Samuel, "Go, lie down; and if he calls you, you shall say, 'Speak, Lord, for thy servant hears.'" So Samuel went and lay down in his place.

I Samuel 3.7-9 RSV

T here is a Thursday morning tradition in this parish, whereby the preacher of the week meets with a small but loyal group of people to discuss the assigned Bible readings for the upcoming Sunday. It is a tradition that has provided a forum for the people and more than one sermon for the preacher. This past week we spent most of our time on the Old Testament reading, in which a voice from heaven awakens twelve year old Samuel and transforms him into a prophet of the Lord. First we exclaimed over the beauty and mystery of the passage; then there was a lull in the conversation as we let the story sink in. Out of the silence one woman began telling about this strange thing that had begun happening to her just lately, how she had been waking up at four in the morning for no reason at all and found it impossible to go to sleep again. A thousand worries consumed her, she said, worries that became trivial as soon as the sun came up but really terrified her in the middle of the night. She did not know what was wrong.

Several older members of the group exchanged knowing looks and announced, somewhat gleefully, "It's age! You're just getting old, that's all!" It turned out that a hefty majority of those present woke up at four in the morning – or three, or two-thirty – and worried. They all had different solutions for their common problem, which they shared with their new compatriot: one walks her dog, one gets up and cooks, one pinches the dead leaves off her houseplants, several read and several more, including myself, make lists. One, bless her soul, sings hymns, but few of us have the memory for that one. What we all had in common was an uneasiness, if not a downright fear, of the night, of the literal power of darkness to make benign things seem bad and bad things seem much, much worse. We could not agree what it was all about, but we agreed that we all heard certain voices in the night, and that they very rarely had anything good to say to us. At four in the morning, my bed can become a coffin. Everything I do not understand crowds in on me – the meaning of life, of death, the fate of the earth, the size of the universe, where God is and what he thinks of the mistakes I have made – they bear down on me without mercy until I manage to numb myself with a prayer, a rhyme, anything mindless and automatic enough to put my panicked brain back to sleep. And I could not tell you what I am more afraid of – that I will hear a voice address me out of the silence or that I will hear absolutely, definitively, nothing at all.

But if we think our own beds can be scary places to be in the middle of the night, imagine poor Samuel sleeping in the temple next to the ark of God. Do you know Samuel? He was his mother Hannah's firstborn son, a miracle baby because everyone, including herself, believed she was barren until the day she went to the temple at Shiloh and prayed for a child. She would do anything to conceive, she said, including give the baby back to God. The old temple priest Eli heard her prayer, blessed it, and true to her word she brought her baby boy Samuel back to Eli as soon as the child was weaned. So it happened that Samuel grew up in the temple at Shiloh, serving Eli – who was ninety years old if he was a day and going blind on top of that – helping the old man with his priestly duties: locking and unlocking the doors of the shrine, keeping the lamp of God filled with oil, scrubbing out pots used to boil the slaughtered sacrifices. It cannot have been a particularly pleasant childhood, even though Eli was kind to Samuel, loving the boy as his own kin, loving the life the child brought into that dark, holy place.

We can only guess what it was like for Samuel, as the faithful brought their burnt-offerings, their sin-offerings, their guilt-offerings to the temple. They were burdened, ashen-faced people, most of them, hauling their stubborn animals up to the altar to be killed. There was a great deal of blood, blood splashed on the altar, blood sprinkled on the veil that separated the Holy of Holies from the rest of the sanctuary. The burning incense did battle with the smell but could not beat it; the place stank, no getting around it. Maybe Samuel tended the cauldron where the sacrificial meat was boiled, or helped Eli locate the portion he was allowed to eat as the temple priest. Maybe Samuel was allowed to feed on some of the scraps himself; there was little else for a growing boy to eat.

At night he lay down by the ark of God, the legendary throne of the invisible king Yahweh that Israel carried into battle at the head of her armies. It was reputed to contain all the sacred relics of the nation's past: a container of manna, Aaron's budded rod, the tablets of the covenant. Sleeping next to it had to be like sleeping in a graveyard, or under a volcano, but Samuel was apparently used to it. Night after night, with his hair full of smoke and the smell of burning fat, he lay down beside it and pulled his cloak around him, trying not to sleep too soundly in case old Eli called him during the night.

Someone *does* call him out of the belly of this particular night, not once but three times, and three times he answers, "Here I am," a variation on "I'm coming," and goes running to see what Eli wants. It is not Eli who has called him, however, but by the time Samuel has awakened him for the third time, Eli has a hunch who it might be. Samuel does not yet know the Lord, we are told, which seems incredible for someone, even a boy of twelve, who has spent his whole life in the Lord's house. There is more to knowing God, it seems, than being in church.

Anyhow, instead of cuffing the boy, Eli rubs the sleep from his eyes and tells Samuel what to say the next time he hears the voice. Say, "Speak, Lord, for thy servant hears," he tells the boy and that is exactly what Samuel does. It is a turning point for him that night, a point on which his whole life turns, not only because of what he hears but also because of what he says: "Speak, Lord, for thy servant hears." He is no longer a child, a temple lackey who comes running at the sound of his name. He has become a young man, a servant of God who is ready to hear what the Lord has to say to him. Compared to the courage that required, sleeping next to the ark was nothing!

The message takes courage to hear as well, because it condemns old Eli's house forever – old blind Eli, the only family Samuel has ever known, damned because his loutish sons have gotten into the bad habit of stealing the best cuts of meat from the temple and taking them home to roast. Eli had warned them but could not make them stop, and now the bill for their wrongdoing has come due. Samuel does not want to tell Eli what he has heard. The next morning he opens up the temple as usual and when Eli calls him he answers as usual, "Here I am," the same words he used to answer Eli *before* his vision. He wants things back the way they were; he wants to remain a child, but Eli knows better. He orders Samuel to tell him all that he has learned, and here there is a peculiar glitch in the Hebrew. "What was it *he* told you," Eli asks, using a plain masculine pronoun that does not presume to know who "he" is. There are plenty of voices that can be heard in the night, it seems, and Eli knows enough to hear the message before he decides whom it is from. The boy balks but

Eli makes it clear that he, like Samuel, is ready to hear the message and Samuel tells him everything. It is the content of the message – the righteousness, the judgment, the bone-rattling power of it that lets Eli know whom it is from, who the "he" is. "It is the Lord," he says. "Let him do what seems good to him." And so it comes to pass that the boy he counted on to be his eyes shows Eli the fiery vision of his own destruction.

Now if that is what happens when you answer voices in the night, then thanks very much but I would just as soon walk the dog. Does anyone really want to hear the voice of the living God? I wonder. I wonder, as I said before, what is worse: to hear it or not to hear it, to face fainting at the power of it or to live oblivious to it, eaten up by the thousand little fears that may prevent its ever getting through. That is what I think about the night terrors, see – sometimes I think all my worrying about the bills, my health, my family, my life, death and the universe, all *that* is what I worry about to avoid saying, in the middle of the night, "Speak, Lord, for thy servant hears." I am so afraid that I will hear something, or that I will not. But all the evidence points toward hearing something, at least eventually. It is our faith and our hope that, since the beginning of time when God's word created heaven and earth, through the word he gave to Abraham and our forebears forever, through the word made flesh in Jesus Christ, God has been speaking to us, and is speaking to us still. But that he has never forced us to hear.

If and when we choose to hear, we could do worse than claim Samuel as our patron saint and to remember his story: how the Lord waited to speak until Samuel declared his readiness to hear; how it took the wisdom of a fellow traveler, old Eli, to help Samuel make sense of what was happening to him and to discern whose voice he heard; how there was no going back once he had heard the word of the Lord; and how that word changed his life forever. It is no invitation for the fainthearted, but it is an invitation we have all been issued just the same. "See that you do not refuse to hear the voice that speaks," Paul writes in Hebrews, and the truth is that it is a voice that is speaking to us always – not only in the middle of the night, although that may be when it is easiest to hear, when all the other voices of our lives are still – and not just in words, although words tend to be easiest for us to understand. The truth is that ever since God decided to speak through a person, the person of his son, his word has come to us in our persons, in our bodies, in all the events of our lives, if only we can learn to hear what they are telling us.

How can we find out? What is God trying, wanting, longing to say to us? His message is different for each of us, as different as our lives. Only our beginnings are the same, our first steps toward finding out, when we are able to summon all our courage, open our mouths and say, "Speak, Lord, for thy servant hears."

BARTIMAEUS
The Courage to See

And they came to Jericho; and as he was leaving Jericho with his disciples and a great multitude, Bartimaeus, a blind beggar, the son of Timaeus, was sitting by the roadside. And when he heard that it was Jesus of Nazareth, he began to cry out and say, "Jesus, Son of David, have mercy on me!" And many rebuked him, telling him to be silent, but he cried out all the more, "Son of David, have mercy on me!" And Jesus stopped and said, "Call him." And they called the blind man, saying to him, "Take heart; rise, he is calling you." And throwing off his mantle he sprang up and came to Jesus.

Mark 10.46-52 RSV

Today's gospel reading is a story about the restoration of sight, among other things, a story about one man who wanted out of his own personal darkness and did everything in his power to gain the light. As such, it is a story that holds clues for those of us who want the same thing, clues that become apparent as we walk around in the story. For the sake of the story, say you are a disciple, any disciple, waking up in Jericho with a knot in your stomach. You did not sleep well; all thirteen of you were bedded down on the same rough pallet and the fellow to your right turned over every twenty minutes all night long. He knows what you know: that Jerusalem is just fifteen miles down the road and, unless you are waylaid, you will be there by dark. You are not sure what will happen there, but from what Jesus has said it sounds grim.

Not that you understand half of what he says. It is harder than you thought, this disciple business. When he asked you to follow him you thought he was headed for success – for high political office, at first, and then – if he is who you think he is – for the very throne of Israel. But lately he has been talking crazy, talking about dying and rising and being a servant. It is not what you expected, and you have thought more than once about going back home. But you love him, and the way he seems to love everyone he meets, never seeing crowds but always seeing people and reaching out to touch them, heal them, make them whole.

It is not long before he is at it again. On your way out of Jericho, with half the town tagging along behind you, you see a blind beggar by the side of the road, rocking back and forth on his heels. Someone groans and says, "It's Bartimaeus again," by which you gather that he is well known, at least by those who support him with their alms. Not to worry, you are thinking, the poor are with us always, when suddenly Bartimaeus' head jerks up and he shouts, "Jesus, son of David, have mercy on me!" Several of the disciples, you included, stop dead in your tracks and look at one another. It is the first time anyone but a demon or a disciple has called Jesus by his title, son of David. How in the world does that blind beggar recognize what no one else can see, that the man on the road in front of him is indeed the Messiah?

But your puzzlement is cut short by the shushing of the crowd. "Be quiet, beggar," someone hisses. "Don't be shameless, Bartimaeus, hustling a rabbi for change. Somebody tell him to shut up." But he will not shut up. "Son of David," he cries again, "have mercy on me!" Jesus hears him this time and stops. "Call him," he says, and the crowd changes its mind about Bartimaeus, scolding him no longer but congratulating him instead, encouraging him to his feet. "Take heart," someone says, "rise up, Bartimaeus, he is calling you! Today must be your lucky day!" But Bartimaeus does not merely rise; he flings off his cloak and springs to his feet, rushing toward the remembered sound of Jesus' voice. He misjudges by a foot or so and plants himself in front of you, his big round eyes rolling in their separate orbits, a look of great expectation on his sunburned face. Someone takes him by the shoulders and turns him slightly, until he is facing Jesus. He is nodding his thanks when Jesus asks him, "What do you want me to do for you?"

Now there is a rhetorical question if you have ever heard one. What does Jesus think he wants, a pair of sunglasses? But no, you know better than that. He is not playing to the crowd; he just wants to hear Bartimaeus say it, say exactly what he wants, exactly how much he believes Jesus can do. So the blind man sums up his heart's desire in six words: "Master," he says, "let me receive my sight," he says, and Jesus replies, "Go your way; your faith has made you well." Just like that, just words – no mud, no spittle, not even a touch – still and all, it is enough. Bartimaeus closes his eyes and when he opens them again they work. "Go your way," Jesus tells him, but he does not go his way, or else he decides on the spot that his way is Jesus' way, because that is the way he chooses, without any way of knowing where it will lead. Still blinking, he chooses the road to Jerusalem in the company of his Lord.

Now that is a splendid story. It is one in which there is no ambivalence; all the verbs are strong and clean – Bartimaeus cries out, springs up, and speaks straight from his heart. His faith is impeccable, and as soon as Jesus says so out loud his eyes are opened and he becomes a disciple, following Jesus on his way as if there is no other way once he can really *see*. It is a perfect story, full of courage and compassion, complete with a happy ending. It is a story about the kingdom of God, and we want it for our own – to encounter Jesus, to be called to him by name, to find the words to tell him what we want and to be healed, illumined, made whole. That is what we want, isn't it? To trade in whatever blindness each of us has got, to trade it in on sight, so that we can see, see ourselves, see our world, see Jesus clearly, without cloud or shadow. That is what we want, isn't it?

It is a metaphorical question, of course, and a good one, but real blindness is something else again. Most of us cannot imagine what it would be like to live in darkness or, having learned to do that, what it would be like suddenly to see, to have to make sense out of color, depth, distance, perspective – all those things we figured out years ago and now take for granted. But what if we did not? What if we had never learned from experience that the sailboat looks small because it is far out on the water? What if we believed we could reach out and take it in our hands, a sailboat just as tiny as it looks? What would it be like to reach out to that exact spot on the horizon right in front of you expecting to touch a toy boat but to close your hands on air, just air? With that tiny sailboat still bobbing there before your eyes, tantalizing you but becoming insubstantial every time your fingers curl around the place where it seems to be? Can you imagine?

In her book *Pilgrim at Tinker Creek,* in a chapter titled "Seeing," Annie Dillard quotes at length from a text called *Space and Sight* by Marius von Senden. What the text is about are the first people in the world to undergo successful cataract surgery. All blind from birth, they suddenly received their sight and were interviewed about what they saw. Their stories are strange and moving; they describe a world we no longer see, describe it like a newborn or an alien might describe it upon seeing it for the first time. One newly sighted girl was shown a batch of photographs and then some paintings by her mother. "Why do they put those dark marks all over them?" she asked. "Those aren't dark marks," her mother explained, "they're shadows."

"Shadows?" the girl asked, and her mother said yes. "That is one of the ways the eye knows that things have shape," she said. "If it weren't for shadows many things would look flat." "Well that's how things *do* look," her daughter answered. "Everything looks flat with dark patches." A second girl was so stunned by the radiance of the world that she kept her eyes shut for two weeks. When she finally opened them she saw only a field of light against which everything seemed to be in motion. She could not distinguish objects, but gazed at everything around her, saying over and over again, "Oh God! How beautiful!"

But not everything was beautiful for these patients. Unable to judge distances, they reached out for things a mile away, or cracked their shins on pieces of furniture they perceived only as patches of color. The world turned out to be much bigger than they had thought, bigger and infinitely more complex. Unable to control it, many fell into depression. Others, having seen themselves for the first time in a mirror, realized how often others had seen them without their awareness or assent. Some became terribly self-conscious about their appearance while others soon refused to go out at all. The distressed father of one young woman wrote her surgeon that his daughter had taken to shutting her eyes when she walked around the house, and that she never seemed happier than when she pretended to be blind again. A fifteen year old boy finally demanded to be taken back to the local home for the blind, where he had left his girlfriend behind. "No, really, I can't stand it anymore," he said. "If things aren't altered, I'll tear my eyes out."

Tear your eyes out? After being rescued from a life in the dark, after being hauled into the light and presented with a world full of color, depth, movement, space, sights? Tear your eyes out? For God's sake, why? *It's just too much.* Too much what? *Too much to see, do, be. It was better before.* Better! How? *Smaller. Quieter. Safer.* But this is what you were made for; you were meant to see. *I would rather not. Besides, the sun hurts my eyes. If you will excuse me I think I will go lie down now.*

Lie down? Take heart! Rise, he is calling you! What will you do? What will any of us do? Because that is what this is all about: to see or not to see – how will we have it? You can stay where you are. You can sit in your familiar dark, where all the edges are rounded off so that you will not hurt yourself, where you need only concern yourself with what is within your reach. You do not want to make a spectacle of yourself, after all, and it probably will not work anyway. No sense getting your hopes up; no sense thinking of yourself as a person who might see. Stay with what you know.

Or you can cry out, spring up, and ask for your heart's desire. Damn the torpedos and good riddance to caution, to propriety, to the fear that keeps you in the dark. Lie down? Take heart! Rise, he is calling you! Are you willing to see or not? And if you are willing, are you willing to see everything there is, the good along with the awful, the lovely along with the monstrous – in yourself, in everyone you meet, in the world? Are you willing to bruise your shins, to learn your way around the obstacles, through the newness of it all, into the mysteries? Are you willing to bruise your heart?

Then go your way, because your faith has made you well. Go your way seeing as if for the first time. Or if, having gained your sight, your own way does not look so appealing anymore, then try another way. It leads to Jerusalem, through a garden, past a cross, to an empty tomb. It is not always scenic, but wait until you see what is there at the end, or should I say *who*. What? You have not been invited? Take heart! Rise up, he is calling you!

MARY
Magnificat

In those days Mary arose and went with haste to the hill country, to a city of Judah, and she entered the house of Zechariah and greeted Elizabeth. And when Elizabeth heard the greeting of Mary, the babe leaped in her womb; and Elizabeth was filled with the Holy Spirit and she exclaimed with a loud cry, "Blessed are you among women, and blessed is the fruit of your womb!"

Luke 1.39-42 RSV

It is almost here. It is almost time. For the four short weeks of Advent we have been waiting in the dark, and some of us for longer than that, waiting for the light of a saviour to come into the world. Our eyes have grown accustomed to the dark; we are good at waiting. We have had a lot of practice. But here it is, almost time. Three days to go and Jesus will once again be born into the world. It is reliable, this reminder of new birth – year after year our Christmas celebration reminds us that God does not stand at a distance, waiting for us to come to him. He has instead come all the way to us, and what the waiting is about is for us to comprehend that, for us to choose the light not only in word but also in deed and truth.

Today we are given a good companion in the last days of our wait – Mary the mother of God, a champion waiter, for whom Christmas was not a reliable reminder of anything but for whom it was a radical, never before, never to be repeated experience of the power of the living God. Today's reading from Luke contains the longest speech she ever makes. It is a song, actually, known through the centuries as the *Magnificat,* which is the first word of the song in Latin. It is one of the church's oldest hymns, and what the song is about is Mary's dawning understanding of what her baby will mean to the world.

Mary is a young girl when she sings her song, thirteen or fourteen, probably, sixteen at the most. She is, like many girls her age, betrothed to a man she hardly knows. It frightens her, to think about leaving home to become his wife, but it does not frighten her nearly as much as some of the other things that have been happening lately. Every time she thinks about that angel her stomach does a flip, the way it used to when her old poppa Joachim tossed her in the air when she was a little girl. The news that angel brought was no news for a little girl, however; it was news that would have set a grown woman to trembling, and Mary wonders if she can bear it, if she can bear a son, a son by God, who will rule over the house of David forever.

The whole scene was so strange – the angel, the whiteness, the voice like bells – she is not even sure it really happened. If it did, what will become of her? As she grows huge with this mysterious angel's child, what will people say? That God chose a teenager, and one already engaged to someone else, to have his baby? Who in the world would believe that? If it really *did* happen. But if it did not happen, well, somehow that is even worse. To go back to the way it was before, back to helping her mother around the house and gossiping with the other girls, back to preparing for her future as she had believed it would be – no, as hard as the other is to believe, it is better than not believing. That is why she answered the angel as she did: "I am the handmaiden of the Lord," she had said to that gleaming, winged thing – how in the world had she thought to say that? "Let it be to me according to your word," she had said, with sudden, perfect confidence.

All the same, she is scared, so scared that she asks her mother and father if she can leave town for a while, and go see her cousin Elizabeth in the uplands of Judah. Elizabeth is much older than she is, older than her mother even, but Elizabeth has never patted her on the head or used that tone of voice that adults use when they speak down to children. No, Elizabeth has always treated her like a full-fledged person, like a friend, and a friend is what she needs. Her parents say yes, that she has been looking a little peaked lately and maybe a change of scenery will do her good. So she goes, and on the journey she has lots of time to worry. What if Joseph denounces her? What if her parents disown her? Never mind the shame – how will she take care of a baby all by herself, with no place to live, no way to get food, no one to help her?

When she finally arrives at Elizabeth's she is a wreck, but at the sight of her beloved cousin she forgets all her woes. Elizabeth is six months pregnant and *gorgeous*. Not gorgeous by ordinary standards, you understand – I mean, she is old – but so full of life that it is hard to see much beyond her joy. Her grey hair is plaited and tied under a kerchief, and as she takes Mary's hands in hers the girl can see dark spots on them, the kind that come with age. Elizabeth's face, too, shows her years, but her eyes are clear and full of light. She sees Mary staring at her big belly and laughs out loud. "God's blessing is on you above all women," Elizabeth says, "and his blessing is on the fruit of your womb."

What? Mary can hardly believe her ears! Has the angel been here too? How does Elizabeth know? And if she knows, why isn't she troubled about it as well? Can't she see what a mess this is going to be, how much explaining there is going to be? But Elizabeth needs no explanation at all; without asking a single question she takes her young cousin in her arms and lets her know that everything, finally, will be all right. Then Mary's stomach does another flip, and she feels a song coming on. That is one of the effects total acceptance has on the soul, you see – your foot starts tapping and mere words will not suffice – you want *music* – a saxophone, a brass band, an entire symphony to accompany your outpouring of gladness. In just such a frame of mind, Mary opens her mouth and begins to sing, *My soul magnifies the Lord, and my spirit rejoices in God my Saviour, for he has regarded the low estate of his handmaiden.*

Without casting any aspersions on Mary's originality, her song contains echoes of a much older song, sung over a thousand years earlier by her kinswoman Hannah. Hannah, like Elizabeth, grew old and despaired of ever having a child until the Lord heard her prayer and blessed her with Samuel. When the miraculous baby boy was born, Hannah took him to the temple and sang too. "My heart rejoices in the Lord, in the Lord I now hold my head high," she sang, "the bow of the mighty is broken, but the feeble have guided themselves with strength." It is a song Mary may have heard before, or else one whose themes are so universal that they crop up again and again whenever God stirs his people's hearts.

What Hannah, what Elizabeth and Mary all have in common, what allows them to sing in harmony, is that they know they have received God's blessing. Each of them has carried that blessing around in her body, kicking and growing until no one who looks at her can miss it. Mary is all but overwhelmed by what is in store for her. *For behold, henceforth all generations will call me blessed.* A little self-centered, you say? Well, she is a teenager, after all, half little girl who has spent the last few days numb with fear. Out from under that fear, she is as excited as if she has been named Queen for a Day. *For he who is mighty has done great things for me, and holy is his name.*

Like the beatitudes in Matthew, this blessedness of Mary's also has two parts: her past humiliation and her future glory. "Blessed are the poor in spirit, those who mourn, who are meek, who are persecuted for righteousness sake" – who wants that half of the equation? But the other half – "for theirs is the kingdom of heaven, for they shall be comforted, shall inherit the earth, shall see God" – now that is the interesting part of blessedness. The trouble is, we cannot have one without the other; they come in matched pairs, and no substitutions, please. So it is with Mary. She has been embarrassed and afraid, the most miserable of the miserable, but God has blessed her in her low estate, has made her a promise she has believed, and that is the living definition of faith, faith that gives substance to our hopes, faith in things not seen.

And his mercy is on those who fear him from generation to generation, Mary's song continues. She fears him, all right; she has proven that. But she also believes what she sees in Elizabeth's eyes, what she has no way of knowing for sure. *He has shown strength with his arm, he has scattered the proud in the imagination of their hearts,* Mary sings, but already the words are turning in her mouth. *He has put down the mighty from their thrones, and exalted those of low degree.* Her, she means, God has put down *her* mighty fears, and has exalted *her,* low as she is. That is what the words mean, isn't it? She is just singing a song about how happy she is, how thankful she is, but then why does she keep seeing *lots* of people as she sings, kings and queens leaving town all by themselves with their crowns flattened in the dust behind them, beggars dressed in brocade, cripples on white stallions. It is all backwards! Everything is upside down!

But the words to her song keep coming, spilling from her lips before she can decide what she thinks about them at all. She is no longer singing the song; the song is singing her, and what music, what verse −! *He has filled the hungry with good things, and the rich he has sent empty away.* Where are these words coming from? She is no politician, no revolutionary; she just wants to sing a happy song, but all of a sudden she has become an articulate radical, an astonished prophet singing about a world in which the last have become first and the first, last. What is more, her song puts it all in the past tense, as if the hungry have *already* been fed, the rich *already* freed of their inordinate possessions. How can that be? Her baby is no bigger than a thumbnail, but already she is reciting his accomplishments as if they were history. Her faith is in things not seen, faith that comes to her from outside herself, and it is why we call her blessed.

On one hand she was just a girl, an immature and frightened girl who had the good sense to believe what an angel told her in what seemed like a dream. On the other hand she was the mother of the son of God, with faith enough to move mountains, to sing about the victories of her son as if he were already at the right hand of his father instead of a dollop of cells in her womb. She was not like us. She *was* like us. She just wanted to thank God for visiting her, but she ended up bearing his son. She just wanted to be blessed in a small way, but she ended up changing the future of the world. She just wanted to sing a happy song, but she ended up singing revolution, singing the Lord's own upheaval and tumult. She was not like us. She *was* like us. When we allow God to be born in us there is no telling, no telling at all, what will come out.

II.
THE FIRSTBORN
OF
ALL CREATION

ADVENT
Saving Space

There is a voice that cries: Prepare a road for the Lord through the wilderness, clear a highway across the desert for our God. Every valley shall be lifted up, every mountain and hill brought down; rugged places shall be made smooth and mountain-ranges become a plain. Thus shall the glory of the Lord be revealed, and all mankind together shall see it; for the Lord himself has spoken. A voice says, "Cry," and another asks, "What shall I cry?" "That all mankind is grass, they last no longer than a flower of the field. The grass withers, the flower fades, but the word of our God endures forevermore."

Isaiah 40.3-8 NEB

For those of us who are counting, today is the second Sunday of Advent. With two down and two to go, we are halfway through this season of waiting, halfway to Christmas and to the coming of Christ as one of us, as part of us. Unlike the culture that surrounds us, the church is in no great hurry to get there. With the wisdom of centuries, our tradition tells us that the journey itself is what we need, as much as finally reaching that shed outside of Bethlehem. It tells us to pause, to take stock, to lie on some hillside a little distant from our destination and watch the stars. It tells us to empty our hearts so that there is room in them for the birth of something new and altogether unforeseen.

"Prepare a road for the Lord," Isaiah says, "clear a highway across the desert for our God." While paving a highway – a sort of landing strip for the Lord – may not be our idea of holy preparation, for a desert nomad it must have seemed like a piece of heaven: for all the valleys to be lifted up and the mountains and hills made low – no more hard climbs or knee-wrenching descents, no bandits down in that gulley or wolves around that bend – no, according to Isaiah, the way of the Lord is flat, and straight, and totally revealed. But that way is apparent only after everything else has passed away, he goes on to say, after the grass has withered, after the flower has faded away and all the glories of the flesh have perished from the face of the earth. Only the word of God will stand forever, he says, which is the prophet's way of telling us that whatever else we get attached to will finally let us down. Only God is forever, he says, only God will never let us down.

That is supposed to comfort us? That everything we know and love is doomed, that the one reliable object of our devotion is the word of a deity so much greater than we are that we know virtually nothing about him? Well, it is only the Old Testament lesson; turn to the other readings of the day and there is bound to be some better news. But there really is not. "The day of the Lord will come like a thief," Peter writes in the epistle, "and then the heavens will pass away with a loud noise, and the elements will be dissolved with fire, and the earth and the works that are upon it will be burned up." Given that fact, he continues, how will we live while we wait? Then John the Baptist appears on the scene like an answer to the question, a rough but utterly sincere character with everything he owns on his back, as wild as the wilderness he has chosen for his pulpit, preaching to everyone who will listen: "Prepare the way of the Lord, make his paths straight . . ." which brings us back to where we started.

So what does it all mean for us? Certainly it is true that most of us are waiting – if not for the day of the Lord then for something else – for true love, for the return of health, for a job that challenges us, for a house to call our own, for peace in our families, in our nation, the world. Most of us are waiting for something, many of us yearning for a "betterness" we cannot name. Like the line from Isaiah, a voice says, "Cry," and we say, "What shall I cry?" The words escape us; all we know is that there must be more and better than this.

That is what makes Isaiah and John our brothers – they too yearn for a betterness they cannot name. For Isaiah it is the revealed glory of the Lord, whatever that high mystery means for him. For John it is the one who will come after him, who is mightier than he. Neither of them knows any details; John cannot even give his hearers a name to listen out for. All that either one of them can proclaim is that the old ways of life are passing away and that new life is on its way. Without the luxury of details, with no concession to our need to know what we are getting ready for, they call us to prepare the way for that new life, to clear away anything that might get in its way, and to wait without knowing when it will come, or what it will look like, or how it will change our lives.

One advantage we twentieth century Christians have over Isaiah and John is that we have heard and believed the story of a particular birth, which gives us reason to talk for a moment about babies, and about what goes into preparing the way for that form of new life in our lives. All fortune-telling and amniocentesis aside, most expectant parents do not know exactly what they are expecting; even if they know the gender of their child they cannot know the rest: what it will look like, be like, how it will change their lives. All they know for sure is that nothing will ever be the same again, and the way most of them go about preparing for that is literally to clear a space – a nursery, or a corner of their own room – a place for this unknown child to become a part of their lives.

Two friends of mine, expecting their second child, looked in vain for a place to park baby number two. After several lengthy discussions it was decided that the husband's study would have to go, his library moved to his office or divided up into smaller bookshelves throughout the house. He loved his library dearly, this friend of mine, but there was new life on the way, and that way had to be prepared. The analogy holds. Whether it is our own baby we are expecting, or the baby Jesus, or a grown-up Lord coming in great power and glory, we are called to prepare the way for new life in our lives, to make room for it by letting go of our old ways, even our old loves, as painful as that may sometimes be. It is either that or prepare ourselves for the news that we have been passed over because there was no room in us.

The title of a book has haunted me throughout my thinking about this sermon, a book assigned for some religion course in college, I think, which I skimmed through and promptly forgot. I do not remember the book but I remember the title: *Wait Without Idols,* it was, and whoever the author was he might as well have been Isaiah, or John, because that is at the heart of each of their messages. The grass withers, the flower fades, heaven and earth will pass away; each of them tells us that it is only when we stop believing in all of these, stop looking to everything that is not God to save us – it is only when we are able to empty our hearts and wait without idols that there is room for God almighty to bring us himself.

What is surprising is how deceptive some of our idols are. I mean, anyone can turn and walk away from a golden calf, and I expect that most of us could toss our savings out the window if we believed our souls depended on it. Those are obvious idols, but what about, say, the idol of *independence* – the belief that everything will be all right if we can just take care of ourselves and not have to ask anyone else to look after us? Or the idol of *romance* – the belief that we can face anything in life if we just have one other person to love us the way we are, and to love in return? Or a variation on that one, the idol of *family* – the belief that if we can just gather around us a close, committed family, our happiness will be unassailable.

Then there is the most deceptive idol of all, the idol of *religion* – the belief that if we go to church and struggle, really struggle to live a life of faith, that our souls will be safe. Name your own idols – the list is long – the idols of *health,* of *friendship,* of *patriotism* – what? You say that these are all good and noble things? Of course they are! How else could they become idols? That is the first criterion of an idol, that it gladden our hearts and nourish our souls, because that is how we learn to believe in it, and depend on it, and finally to cling to it as the only possible source of life for us. The only problem is that as long as our hearts and souls are full of what we *know* will sustain us, we have lost our ability to receive the as-yet unknown things that God has in store for us. We are full up; there is no room at the inn. God is looking for a nursery, but we are inside our study with the door closed.

During Advent we are invited to come out, to let go, to open up – not to forsake the things we love and want for our lives but to forsake them as *idols* – to learn to hold them lightly, without clinging, and to be willing to give them up when it becomes clear that they are taking up too much room. Because during Advent we are invited to prepare the way for something new and unknown in our lives, brought to us in person by the living God. So what will it be for you? What might new life mean for you? But what has to go first? What is taking up too much room?

It is all right if we do not know all the answers, because that too is what Advent is about: preparing a place for something new in our lives, for new life in us, and then waiting without knowing, waiting with nothing but faith, hope and love for company in the stillness that teaches us how completely we live at God's mercy, a mercy that promises everything, that promises the advent of God himself to those who have saved him room.

CHRISTMAS
Decked Out in Flesh

For to us a child is born, to us a son is given; and the government shall be upon his shoulder, and his name will be called "Wonderful Counselor, Mighty God, Everlasting Father, Prince of Peace."

Isaiah 9.6 RSV

Tonight the wait is over. Tonight is the night when all our preparations have been made – or abandoned – and we are here to settle into a mystery, to follow a star to Bethlehem and join the crowd that is gathering around a manger. Tonight is the night, when even the cynics among us take a sabbatical and we all suspend disbelief, believing if only for this night that God is born among us and everything is possible. Tonight is the night, when with all our singing we wish Jesus a happy birthday and us too, all of us who claim him as our Lord. Because it is our birthday too, somehow, a night when we come here to celebrate everything that has been born in us because of this singularly wonderful child.

Tonight is the night, and everything is in place. We know the carols, we know the readings, we know the whole story so well we can tell it by heart – the star, the shepherds, the angel, the baby. What kind of baby? Well, that depends largely on you. A perfect baby, at any rate, the kind you find in *Art Masterpieces of the World* or on the highest shelf of your imagination: a pink-cheeked faintly glowing baby, wrapped in candescent flannel with a silk banner above his head that reads, "Joy to the world. Peace on earth. Goodwill toward men." A God-child at the center of your favorite Christmas card.

Well, tonight is the night to do him and do yourself a favor. Reach into that picture and take him into your arms, a bundle about as heavy as a sack of flour, his head a little bruised from his rough entrance to the world. Examine his tiny fingernails, count his toes, scrape the fleck of cow manure off his cheek and say to yourself, "This is God in my arms." Smell Mary's milk on his breath, feel the damp warmth spreading through his swaddling clothes and repeat it. "I am holding God in my arms. This is what God has decided to look like, and all for the love of me." Shocking, isn't it? To behold the king of the universe unable to turn over on his back without assistance, utterly dependent upon the kindness of his creatures? Sure, we know the story by heart, but do we have any earthly idea what it means? What kind of child is this, and what is God's message for us this night?

In the first place, a baby is – in the best of worlds – evidence that a love affair has taken place, and that is certainly the case with this particular child. God has loved humankind from the moment he thought us up, but the relationship has always been a rocky one. In the beginning God figured paradise would be enough for us; he gave us everything and hoped for the best; but we wanted more than everything – we wanted to possess him too and wound up banished, ushered from the garden by two angels with flaming swords. "So all right," God said, "You need something more concrete. Let us make a covenant together, you and me. I will be your God and you will be my people. You be faithful to me and I will be faithful to you." But we were not faithful; we doubted God at every turn and protested that we did not know what he wanted from us.

"So all right," God said, "You need some guidelines. Here are ten commandments it would please me for you to follow. I will write them down on rocks so you do not lose them, and by the way they are for your own good. Keep them and you will be happy." But we broke them, in more ways than one, and God took yet another step in our direction. "Let me simplify the covenant," he said. "Love me and love your neighbor, just those two, and never mind the rocks. I will write these two on your hearts so they are not so hard to carry around." But even that was not enough. The history of our love affair with God is the repeated story of our frailty and his forgiveness. Every time the distance between us has threatened to end the relationship, it is he who has stepped across the breach, taking on more and more of the burden, until with the birth of a baby he accepted it all.

"Put the old covenant on hold," God says tonight through this Christ child. "I have a new kind of covenant in mind, harder for me but easy for you: from now on you do not have to come to where I am, however much I would like you to. I am so crazy in love with you that I will come all the way to where you are, to be flesh of your flesh, bone of your bone. I will do it all, and all you have to do is believe me – that I love you the way you are, love you enough to become one of you, and that I love you to death." It is a scandalous move on God's part. Where is his majesty? Where is his pride? What makes him believe we will still respect him after he has laid himself bare like that? He is a shameless lover, willing to reduce himself to a helpless thing in diapers if it will help us love him the way he loves us.

This is the mystery we come to worship tonight – the mystery of the incarnation, the mystery of a God so in love with us that he came to be one of us, and it is something we know so well we are apt to forget that we do not understand it at all. If we did, we would probably behave more like Sharon, a five year old girl quoted by author John Shea who wound up her own version of the Christmas story by asking her listeners this question: "Then the baby was borned," she said, "And do you know who he was?"

"The baby was God," she whispered and leaped into the air, twirled around and dove into the sofa, where she covered her head with pillows. It was, Shea says, the only proper response to the Good News of the Incarnation, and those of us without pillows over our heads may wonder if we have really heard it yet.

So that is the first part of tonight's message. This baby is a love-child, in whom God shows us just how far he will go to be held in our arms. The second part of the message is that in doing so, he has forever blurred the distinction between the holy and the ordinarily human. He could have come among us as a celestial being, say, or a mighty emperor, in some form clearly superior to ours and beyond our reach. He would have been easier to recognize that way, and we could have kept our distance from him. But God chose to come among us as a child, and a poor child at that. Choosing flesh, he chose the lowest human common denominator and in doing so left us no escape from his presence. That is why it is so important tonight to let the star show us a real child, to believe that what Mary and Joseph got was no Hallmark baby but a belching, squalling infant who kept them up nights for weeks, and that in choosing to make his entrance in such an ordinary way, God showed us that flesh and blood, dirt and sky, life and death were good enough for him. More than that, he hallowed them, made them holy by taking part in them, and left us nothing on earth we can dismiss as trivial or unknown to him.

Legend has it that one Christmas eve long ago Saint Francis and his ragged followers staged a small nativity play. Gathering their materials from the garbage bins of Assisi, they made costumes out of rags and hammered a small manger from some old boxes they had found. They stuffed it with hay swept from the streets and into the cradle Francis placed a discarded wooden doll, a *bambino* some child had grown tired of. Later that night, the legend goes, Francis picked up the doll and as he spoke about the mystery of the word made flesh, the baby in his arms came to life. Dive for the couch! Hide in the pillows! Things that cannot be have come to pass this night: God has come among us as a lover and a child, and every ordinary, created thing has become transparent with his glory. There is gold in the straw and myrrh in the dung on the floor; the cows smell of frankincense, the dogs bark hosanna and the star shows seekers from every corner of the earth where to look for God – not up in the heavens, but down, down in the gorgeous muck and hubbub of the world.

For tonight at least let us revel in the light of that star, beneath which the ordinary becomes holy and the holy ordinary, beneath which it becomes exceedingly clear that there is nothing more we must do or be to be loved by God and that we are in fact already loved beyond our wildest dreams for being exactly the way we are. For tonight at least let us believe that on this first day of Christmas, and on the second, and on every day of our lives what our true love sends to us is his holy self, decked out in flesh like ours, and that if we have the wisdom to embrace the everyday stuff of our lives then it is God himself who is born in our arms. The star shines on for those with eyes to see.

EPIPHANY
Sacramental Mud

During a general baptism of the people, when Jesus too had been baptized and was praying, heaven opened and the Holy Spirit descended on him in bodily form like a dove; and there came a voice from heaven, "Thou art my Son, my Beloved; on thee my favor rests."

Luke 3.21-22 NEB

It was over a year ago that my husband and I followed the advice of a friend and traveled to Calistoga, California, for our first mudbath. For those of you who are innocent of mudbathing I would like to describe the experience, while you wonder what it can possibly have to do with the baptism of our Lord. First we selected a spa – the Golden Days Spa, as I recall – and arrived at the appointed hour to meet a red-headed young man who introduced himself as our M.B.A. "That stands for Mud Bath Assistant," he explained as he handed us two terrycloth robes and showed us where to shower. Several moments later he led us to a tiled room with a whirlpool bath in one corner, an assortment of shovels, rakes and hoses in the other, and two tiled tubs in the center, full of steaming black mud.

It was, he said, a combination of volcanic ash and peat moss, maintained at a steady temperature of 110 degrees. "Just get in and cover yourselves up as best you can," he said, "then I'll come in and finish the job." That sounded ominous, but we obeyed, dipping in first a toe, then a foot, while a loud parental voice boomed in my head, "That is *mud,* you fool! You are about to lie down in a tub full of *mud!*" But lie down I did, and it was like nothing I have ever felt. It was hot, and heavy, and smelled like the kind of bogs dinosaurs used to get stuck in. I found a rock underneath me with one hand and a stick with the other. I wondered where exactly this mud had been before it was around me. Then the M.B.A. came back in and raked more mud over us until we were both covered up to our chins. At first we laughed, but as the heat and weight got to us we grew more solemn, and I at least was conscious as never before of what it was like to be buried alive, to be lying naked under pounds and pounds of real dirt. *From dust you came and to dust you shall return,* I thought. *This is what it means.* My heart began to pound, partially from the heat but also from the fresh reminder of my mortality.

It was a long time before the M.B.A. stuck his head in the door again and told us to get up and shower. Eagerly we began to unearth ourselves from our little graves, lifting one limb after the other out of the mud. But it did not let go easily; as I raised myself up the mud sucked me back down again and by the time I finally stood on my own two feet again I felt as though I weighed a ton. Covered with mud I made my way to the shower and all but wept as the cool water poured over me. I had skin again! I had returned from the land of the dead and was washed, made clean by living waters! *If I ever get to design my own religion,* I thought, *this is how we will do baptisms.*

See? It did have something to do with today's reading from Luke, which is his account of the baptism of Jesus, which is the story about how Jesus joined us in the mud. It is a story that each of the evangelists tells a little differently. Mark tells it urgently: *immediately* after Jesus came out of the water he saw the heavens *torn* open and the spirit, like a dove, descending upon him. Matthew is much more academic by comparison. According to him, John the Baptist and Jesus engage in a theological debate about who should baptize whom before John relents and dips Jesus in the Jordan like any other Galilean. The fourth gospel, on the contrary, is so defensive about Jesus' purity that it does not mention his baptism at all. It might give the reader the wrong impression, see, to show Jesus being washed alongside ordinary sinners. So in John's telling of the story John the Baptist testifies that he saw the Spirit come down from heaven and rest upon Jesus like a dove, but he does not mention that Jesus happened to be standing in the river Jordan at the time.

And then there is Luke, whose account is likewise eccentric. Just before he describes Jesus' baptism in detail, Luke tells us that Herod has put John the Baptist in prison, so that there is in his story no mention of the Baptizer at all. That is because the spotlight is not on who did the baptizing or even on who was baptized, but on a dove and a voice from heaven: "Thou art my Son, my Beloved; on thee my favor rests." But let us back up a little, to the day or so before the great event occurred. The people were in expectation – "on the tiptoe of expectation," according to one translation – wondering if John were the Christ. He was certainly an unusual man, fierce and uncompromising. He spoke with authority, pronounced judgment with authority, and the very fact that he found everything wanting was enough to convince some that he was indeed the Messiah. They came out to be baptized by him and he called them a brood of vipers, warning them that if they did not produce good fruit they would be cut down and thrown on the fire to burn. If he was mad, they reasoned, he must be of God, but when John heard that he got even madder.

"I baptized you with water," he said, "but he who is mightier than I is coming, whose shoes I am not worthy to untie, and he will baptize you with the Holy Spirit and with fire." Uh-oh, the people thought, knowing enough about what he meant to be afraid. The Holy Spirit of God was one thing, sweeping across your soul like a wind from heaven, but fire – well, that was something else altogether. Fire was a purifier, that much was for certain, and you might be a better person for having gone through it, but make no mistake: it was going to hurt, and the scars would be ugly. Imagine the people's surprise, then – imagine John's surprise – when who should show up but Jesus, no ax-wielding arsonist but a gentle carpenter whom the Holy Spirit chooses for a roost, whom God claims for his own beloved son. And many did not believe it, as many do not quite believe it even now, because they found it easier to believe in an angry God than in a loving one.

But what was Jesus doing there in the first place? John made it clear that his baptism was for sinners, sinners who came to him to be washed in the waters of repentance and rose from them to go and sin no more. What need did Jesus have of a bath like that? He was, according to every eyewitness, a man set apart by his sinlessness. He had nothing to repent of and nothing to be forgiven for. How much more appropriate it would have been if he had walked up to John and said, "Thank you for all your preparations, my friend. I will take over now." But that is not what he did. In fact, there is not a single story in all of the gospels about Jesus baptizing anyone. His disciples baptized; Paul baptized; but Jesus did not, because he did not come to claim power but to give it away.

So he did not take over John the Baptist's ministry. Instead, he got in line with a whole crowd of sorry-looking people and took his turn in the Jordan like everyone else. Nothing unusual so far. It was after his baptism, as he was praying, that the remarkable thing happened: heaven opened – the clouds parted, white light poured through, and a figure that looked a lot like a bird but most of all like something straight from the heart of God – it settled on Jesus as a voice from somewhere other than earth told what it meant. "You are my son, my love," the voice said, "and I am very pleased with you." What words! What acceptance! They would have been fine enough coming from anyone on earth, but for them to come from heaven –! Still, what had Jesus done that was so pleasing? It was the very beginning of his ministry;

all he had done so far was to say yes to it, oh – and to join humankind in the Jordan. Yes, he did that. He joined us in the mud, and a voice from heaven declared, "You are my beloved son, and I am very pleased with you."

Now anyone standing around who knew the Bible could probably have told you that when God said that, he was quoting himself. "You are my beloved son" – that part was from the second psalm, a coronation psalm used to proclaim a king. But the second part, "with you I am well pleased" – that part was a direct quote from this morning's Old Testament lesson from Isaiah, in which God talks about his suffering servant, his chosen one who will redeem the world but only by sacrificing himself. Put the two together and you have a God-given description of who Jesus is and what he has come to do, a public declaration of what his ministry is to be about.

So that is part of what happens in today's story. Jesus goes into the waters of the Jordan a carpenter and comes out a Messiah. He is the same person, but with a new direction. His being is the same, but his doing is about to take a radical turn. That is, by the way, not a bad definition of repentance: to turn around, to go another way, God's way. So in that sense, it is true enough that Jesus repented; if not of any sin, then of going his own quiet way in peace. He went into the waters of baptism his own person, a private man, and came out God's person, a public figure at the center of controversy for the rest of his short life. But that still does not answer our question: why baptism? Why not an eloquent speech or a simple ordination to mark this great passage in Jesus' life? It is as big a mystery as the Christmas mystery of the incarnation. Why did he become human when he could have stayed God? Why was he baptized with us when he could have stayed on the banks of the Jordan and supervised? Why does he come to us where we are, over and over again, when he could save himself the grief, the pain, the death, by insisting that we come to him where he is?

Because he loves us, that is why; because he is, unbelievably, pleased with us, and because he has come to lead us through the waters of life and death into life eternal. It has never been his style to shout directions to us from some safe place of his own. He has always led us from within our midst, joining us in the water, in the mud, in the skin to show us how it is done. If he had not been baptized, now *that* would have been sin for him – if he had chosen to separate himself from us as he had every right to do. But he did not. He took the plunge right along with the rest of us and so it came to pass that he who was without sin was baptized in the river Jordan to avoid the sin of standing apart from us.

He is our servant and our Lord, and he never asks us to go anywhere he has not been first. From dust to dust and ashes to ashes, from the cradle through the waters of baptism to the grave he knows what we are up against and has showed us how to live so that life never ends: choosing to go God's way, choosing whatever will bring us closer together, and above all choosing the things of earth – doves, water, mud, skin, love – to carry out the purposes of heaven.

PALM SUNDAY
Blood Kin

Then Jesus went with them to a place called Gethsemane, and he said to his disciples, "Sit here, while I go yonder and pray." And taking with him Peter and the two sons of Zebedee, he began to be sorrowful and troubled. Then he said to them, "My soul is very sorrowful, even to death; remain here, and watch with me."

Matthew 26.36-38 RSV

There is a legend, that on his famous trip to the Far East, the explorer Marco Polo was seized and brought before the dreadful conquerer Genghis Khan. Desperate for conversation, he began to tell the Khan the story of Jesus, straight out of the gospel according to Saint Matthew. The Khan liked the story and listened attentively, much to his storyteller's relief, but as Marco Polo came to the events of Holy Week and told of Jesus' betrayal, trial, scourging and crucifixion, his fearsome host became more and more agitated. As soon as Marco Polo pronounced the words, "And Jesus cried again with a loud voice and yielded up his spirit," the Turk exploded. "What did the Christians' God do then?" he demanded. "Did he send his thousands of legions from heaven to smite and destroy those who had so treated his son?" Polo's answer clearly disappointed the Khan, who remained unconverted, but I tell the tale to remind us how inured we have become. Of *course* God did not send any legions; that is not how the story goes. Jesus died on the cross for our sins, and three days later was raised from the dead to show us that all who believed in him would not perish but have eternal life. Period. Silly Khan. Silly anyone who does not know the story. But how well do we really know the story, we who have always known it? We have heard it a thousand times, but always with the last page, the victory in mind. Who can remember the first time? Who can recall the suspense of the story, the shock, the outrage, the grief, the wonder?

That is what we are asked to do this Holy Week, beginning today. Today we are asked to endure the story of the death of Jesus in living color, in gory detail, and in the week to come we are asked to walk with him and his disciples every step of the way – with no knowledge of Sunday, no knowledge of empty tombs or resurrections, but only of gathering doom, and threatening weather, and the smell of death all around. We are asked to forget what we know, and to follow our Lord to his wretched death without a clue what will happen next, because it is only then, when we have shared even a splinter of his cross, that he has anything more to offer us. It is our final Lenten discipline and it is hard, extremely hard, not only because we do know what will happen next, and because the story is as familiar to us as the shape of our own hands – but also because it is so very painful, if we make ourselves stop and notice it like someone who is seeing it all happen for the first time.

What a catalogue of griefs it is, this morning's gospel; what an account of thorough failure at home and abroad, with friends and family as well as with those watching from a distance, beginning with Gethsemane. The word means "olive press," a device in which the fruit of the gnarled olive tree is crushed to produce fragrant oil. Jesus has just come from supper with his friends, where he has passed a cup of wine around and called it his blood. It might as well be a winepress in that garden, for the fruit of his short life is being crushed in fulfillment of the scriptures. Who knows what will come of it? "Father, if it be possible, let this cup pass from me." His disciples have seen Jesus sad before, but never afraid. He has always been their leader: the teacher, the rabbi, the miracle worker. What has come over him? Something dreadful, that he should turn to them for help. "Watch with me," he asks them, but they cannot keep their eyes open. It is late, and the Passover meal was sumptuous. So they sleep, certain that their chief remains in control, sure that no one can pull a fast one on the son of God. He wakes them before the torches do, torches and a tangle of angry voices. Now the failures follow in quick succession: Judas' betrayal, the disciples' desertion, Peter's denials, the court's conviction, the crowd's choice of Barabbas.

And so it comes to pass that Jesus is scourged and hung upon the cross like a scarecrow. I did not know the meaning of the word "scourge" until I visited the Shroud of Turin exhibit recently, where there was a scourge on display – a fistful of long leather strips, with a sharp metal spike knotted in the end of each one. The shroud itself bore witness to what a scourge can do; it was soaked with blood, and if there is any connection between that cloth and Jesus, then there was not a piece of unflayed flesh left on his bones when he died. He hung upon the cross, literally, a scarlet man, whose life's blood poured out of him in streams. But even at that he refused the blindfold, so to speak; he refused the cheap wine laced with myrrh that might have numbed him and let him die in a haze. He refused it, and chose instead to stay alive with everything left in him, to feel everything he could feel, including the worst possible human pain, until he could feel no longer. If he asks us to do the same, it is because he knows there is no way around pain, only through it. That knowledge cost him a great deal, cost him so much that his last words in this life were, "My God, my God why?" And that is as far as we get, for this week at least.

If you are anything like me, the almost unbearable pain is the suspicion of my own participation in this gruesome drama. It is the custom in many churches to read the Passion narrative out loud on Palm Sunday, with someone playing Pilate's part, someone else playing Peter's, and the crowd – the congregation – playing itself. Our lines in the script are labeled "All," and what we are given to say is, "He deserves death," "Let him be crucified," and, with dripping sarcasm, "Hail, King of the Jews!" The first time I read them out loud I feared for my life. "Crucify him!" I whispered, meaning to shout, and the words all but gagged me. Like all latter day saints blessed with retrospective piety, I could not believe that I would have said such a thing. But what are the odds? The odds are that I, like Judas, like Peter, like all the others who supped with Jesus and then abandoned him – the odds are that I too would have turned tail and run for my life. Do you need proof? Then forget that Thursday in Gethsemane. Examine last Thursday in Atlanta. Did I love God with my whole heart? Love my neighbor as myself? Recognize Christ in everyone I met? Of course not. I went about my business, which is chiefly the business of self-preservation, as surely as Peter insisted, "I do not know the man."

But the point of all this is not to rub salt in my wounds, or yours. Of course we betray him; of course we are sinners; of course we fall short of the glory of God. The most dreadful line in our script today is, "His blood be on us and our children," as of course it is, but the very great, the very mysterious and most holy surprise is that Jesus takes that murderous fact and turns it into the occasion of our kinship with him. Let me speak plainly: everything we have spoken of up to this point is celebrated in the sacrament of holy communion, in which we are invited to eat the Lord's flesh and drink his blood. Is that sacrament something else we have learned by heart, so that we no longer really notice it? The *children* notice. During one of my first stints as a chalice bearer, I tipped the cup toward the lips of a cherubic six year old. "The blood of Christ," I said, as quietly as I could, "the cup of salvation."

"Yuck!" she said, pushing the cup away, "I don't want any." But who can blame her? Who, without benefit of theological metaphor, would willingly drink from a cup full of anyone's blood? By now she has grown up, and has learned that it is only ruby port in the cup, and someone has explained to her not to worry about the blood part, that what it is really all about is sharing in the life of Christ. That is true enough; but equally true is her first, fully natural, fully sensible response of *repulsion*. What, we may wonder, *what* did Jesus have in mind with a supper of his body and blood?

For any first century Jew the image had to be an awful one. God had been so clear in his revelations to the prophets, that he took no pleasure in blood sacrifice, that he turned his back on the ritual slaughter of animals and innocents. The images of eating flesh and drinking blood were reserved for one's worst enemies, for those whom you wished dead, or who wished you dead. How Judas must have squirmed in his seat, sure that the whole scene was being acted out to point the finger at him. But the whole idea was, from anyone's perspective, a scandal – that Jesus should bless those symbols of death and persecution and then ask his friends to accept them as symbols of life and fellowship. It was crazy. It was a sad, bad joke. Or to look at it another way, it was as if he already knew what was about to happen to him, already knew that in the end he would walk alone to his death, and it was his way of showing them ahead of time that he bore them no malice, that his love for them was stronger than death, and that he required no more of them than to be who they were, and to be loved by him.

It was, I say, as if he knew the truth about them, and about us – that we are amateurs at love, that we do fall asleep on him, and fail to answer his call for our help, and abandon him when the going gets tough. That is half the story, but the other half is that knowing the truth about us does nothing to diminish his love of us. That is the whole story of the Last Supper, and Holy Week, and the Passion – whether or not we recognize our participation in Christ's death, the sacrament of holy communion lets us know that he does, and in it he also lets us know – gently, insistently, radically – that we are forgiven before we ever turn away from him. Which means that nothing can separate us from him, not guilt, not failure, not sorrow or remorse. All of those have been blessed ahead of time and turned into the food and drink of forgiveness, and what might have been just a bloody tragedy, and a bloody meal to commemorate it, has become for us the heart of our faith – the story and symbols of our co-inherence with our Lord, our life within his life, our membership in his body. And because he forgives us before we ever turn away, the road back to him is always open. There is nothing finally in our way.

Let us, then, keep him company this week, and stay awake with him, and, forsaking our own comfort, walk with him as far as we can. Today's gospel story ends bitterly; it leaves Christ dead upon the cross, and while everything in us wants to rush to the Easter affirmation that he is also risen and he will come again, for this week at least we are asked to stay with him where he is, to share his story and his pain like someone who is experiencing it all for the first time – like a Genghis Khan, like a six-year-old child – and to be hurt by it, and healed by it, and amazed.

EASTER
The Familiar Stranger

So they drew near to the village to which they were going. He appeared to be going further, but they constrained him, saying, "Stay with us, for it is toward evening and the day is now far spent." So he went in to stay with them. When he was at the table with them, he took the bread and blessed, and broke it, and gave it to them. And their eyes were opened and they recognized him; and he vanished out of their sight.

Luke 24.28-31 RSV

This is the stuff of romance, this account of Christ's appearance on the road to Emmaus. No sooner do the two disciples recognize their beloved than he disappears from their sight, as Brigadoon vanishes into the mist of a Scottish hillside, as the handsome knight reaches out to touch his beautiful, cursed princess just as she turns into a hawk and flies away. Our own stories may have less magic in them, but many of us know what it is like – all of a sudden, if only for a moment, to realize that our greatest hope, our dearest love, is standing right in front of us, but no sooner do we recognize it than it is gone. Oh, cruel fate! Why can't we hang on to the things we love? Why won't they stay put, stay within our reach, stay the way they are? Stay with us!

Like the first service on Easter morning, for instance: after the long silence and darkness of Lent, the small fire kindled before dawn on the lawn of the church, a hundred of us who carried candles into the dim church, where we heard all the old stories of God's saving grace and then, with the rising of the sun, watched as the black shroud was snatched from the altar cross, to the riotous sound of bells, loud alleluias, as the lights went up full and the church was filled with lilies, with wings, with gladness and singing and a joyous recognition: "Alleluia," we cried, "The Lord is risen! The Lord is risen indeed!" Why can't it always be like that? Why do we ever have to come down off that mountain?

The disciples wondered the same thing. They wanted Jesus with them, wanted him nearby in case questions needed answering, in case wounds needed healing; they wanted him where they could lean on him, and follow his lead, and altogether bask in his presence. They had a Lord they could see, and hear, and touch, and they liked it that way. Oh, and wouldn't we like it too – a God with skin, with a smell, with a humanity we could hang on to. Stay with us! Stay, Stay. But he died; he went away, and although several of them saw him later, it was never the same again. "They have taken my Lord away and I do not know where they have laid him," weeps Mary outside his tomb, and indeed she never sees *her* Lord again, but sees instead the risen Lord, the death-defying Messiah, so changed that she does not recognize him in the garden, as Simon Peter does not recognize the stranger on the shore, as these two disciples do not recognize the foreigner who joins them on the road to Emmaus. And what chaos it creates, this resurrection of his. Where can the disciples turn now for guidance? Who will tell them what to do next? How can the body of the faithful live without its head, its heart? He comes and goes, walking in through closed doors and out them again, unswayed by their pleas that he stay. Stay with us! Stay. Stay.

But he will not stay, that is the truth of it – not for them and not for us – he will not stay put, stay the same, stay with us. "Stay!" That is our chorus, but his refrain is, "Follow!" *Follow me,* he says over his shoulder as he moves out into the world, broadcasting his Holy Spirit, blending into the crowd of humanity so well that, if we choose to go after him, we must search every face on the off chance that it might be his.

Those are our choices, it seems: we can beg him to stay with us or we can follow him. We can plead with him to stay put and, when he does not, we can sit alone with our memories and perhaps even make some up – whatever will fuel our nostalgia and grief, which are all we will have left. We can do that or we can go after him, plunge into the crowd right behind him and, although the sea of faces that parted for him closes back in on us, still we can catch a glimpse of him here and there, in the face of a gardener, a foreigner, a stranger on the road. If we are thorough we will handle each person we meet with care just in case it is he; if we are diligent we will wash some feet along the way, feed some hungers, soothe some sorrows, just in case they are his. You can never be too sure.

Of course, the problem with this approach is that we are likely to forget exactly what he looked like. With so many faces to sort through, some of the details are likely to get lost. Were his eyes brown, or a faded blue like that old woman's? Was his complexion smooth, or wrinkled like that weary-looking fellow's? Did he walk straight, or a little stooped, like that boy with the crutch? Chances are, that in looking for him and wanting so much to find him, that we will begin to see a little bit of him in everyone we meet. So the problem with this approach is that the whole human race may begin to bear a family resemblance to the one we seek, so that when he walks up to us in his completeness we do not recognize him. Or at least not at first.

THANKSGIVING
Mixed Blessings

You must remember all that road by which the Lord your God has led you these forty years in the wilderness to humble you, to test you to discover whether or not it was in your heart to keep his commandments. He humbled you and made you hungry; then he fed you on manna which neither you nor your fathers had known before, to teach you that man cannot live by bread alone but lives by every word that comes from the mouth of the Lord.

Deuteronomy 8.2-4 NEB

There is something so appropriate about being in church this Thanksgiving Thursday, but also something paradoxical – that we should all drop what we are doing, halt all our preparations for a feast, and come to this still, far place to share a wafer of bread and a swallow of wine. What is it all about, this mere suggestion of a meal? And what does it have to do with the spread that awaits most of us at home? To the naked eye there is no resemblance at all between the two meals, but in truth they are twins, for both are about the giving of thanks. For the ancient Hebrews the word was *berakah,* a blessing offered over food and drink; for the Greeks the word was *eucharist* or thanksgiving, a word that has come to mean what Christians do around their altars – holy communion, holy eucharist, the Lord's supper. Without too much etymological violence, then, Thanksgiving Day becomes Eucharist Day, a day when we are called to offer thanks to God for the whole of our lives.

Which is not always an easy thing to do. Through a quirk in scheduling, this is the second Thanksgiving sermon I have preached in a row. When I sat down to write this one and remembered everything that has happened since the last one, I was overcome by how much sorrow there has been – lingering deaths and tragically quick ones; street people lined up night after night for a bologna sandwich and a place on the floor; old marriages and new ones speeding to an end; people assassinated for their politics, their religion, their looks; the faces of starving children pleading from magazine covers – say what? Say thank you? Think again.

Last week I found a bumper sticker that summed it all up, an example of the laugh-until-you-cry school of humor. "Life is hard," it says, "Then you die." I bought another one at the same time, that reads, "You have obviously mistaken me for someone who cares." As I was showing them around yesterday to great hilarity, one perceptive person declined to laugh, cocked her head, and said, "Have you had a hard week?" I have had a hard *year,* and not just me; the world has had a hard year, no harder than most but hard nonetheless. Three weeks ago, after four hard deaths and four grief-filled funerals in a row, I had a falling out with God, a dark day of the soul, if you will, and more or less asked him what good he was. An impertinent question, I know, but heartfelt. My answer was a fifth death – a young man at whose wedding I had officiated just a month before, who was killed when his car was hit broadside by a train. His bride called and asked me to bury him. I did not tell her I did not know how, that I had never done a funeral before. I just took a deep breath and went to be with her, and within two hours her family and I had handled everything: the newspaper notice, the church, the altar guild, the funeral home, the organist.

All that was left was the service itself. I had no idea what I would say, no idea whether my voice would hold up. It did not seem important. The appointed hour came, the church filled, the family and I met the coffin outside and followed it to the altar steps. My voice *did* crack and it was *not* important. Just remember three things, one of my colleagues had told me: you are there to give thanks for his life, to tell him goodbye, and to commend him to God. *We are here to give thanks for his life,* I thought, *how strange.* He is dead at thirty, and we are here to give thanks for his life; not to argue that it should have been longer, or easier, or different in any number of ways; just to give thanks for what there was of it, to be glad we knew him and to say a blessing over as much life as he had before commending him to God.

So that is what we did, and once we did everything changed, for me at least. I have searched for adequate words to describe what changed and have failed, but it had something to do with trusting God to be God and to run the world. I gave up my notions of the way life ought to be and recognized the obvious: that people do die, sooner or later, for all sorts of reasons, but that they never die to the love of God, and that in between the cracks of that Great Truth there are a thousand reasons to say thank you to God and to one another, for the gift of every moment of life and love in this world and the next. Annie Dillard says it more piquantly in her Pulitzer Prize-winning book *Pilgrim at Tinker Creek*. "I think that the dying pray at the last not 'please' but 'thank you,'" she writes, "as a guest thanks his host at the door. Falling from airplanes the people are crying thank you, thank you, all down the air . . ."

It is not a new idea, giving thanks for apparent tragedy and trusting God to be God. Three thousand years ago the Jews formulated blessings – *berakoth* – for every circumstance of their lives. Come weal or woe, they had a blessing. If it were good news, then "Blessed be he who is good and does good." If it were bad news, then "Blessed be the judge of truth." As far as they were concerned, humankind had a duty to pronounce a blessing on the bad in life as well as the good, because all life came from God. "It is forbidden," says the Talmud, "to taste of this world without a blessing." But that is not news, is it? Not to anyone who has broken bread and lifted the cup at this altar, where what we give thanks for is the life, and death, and life of Jesus Christ? We do not bless just the good parts here and curse the rest. No; whenever we gather for eucharist, for thanksgiving, what we toast is the whole of our Lord's life, the defeats along with the victories, the gentle birth alongside the violent crucifixion, the sleepless night in Gethsemane alongside the empty tomb on Easter morning. Because in retrospect, in faith, we believe that it is all a single tapestry, and that the removal of a single thread diminishes the whole creation.

Our challenge this Thanksgiving morning is to see our own lives the same way, to learn how to give thanks at this altar not only for the mixed blessings of Christ's life but also for our own, to say "thank you" for the whole mess, the things we welcome as well as the things we would risk our souls to escape. The image that comes to mind is the ritual we have developed around the reading of scripture as part of our worship in this place. The reader finishes the reading, pauses for a moment to let it sink in, and says, "The word of the Lord." Then it is the congregation's turn to accept that word by responding, "Thanks be to God," which is an easy and a natural thing to say when the lesson has been about God's goodness towards us. But how about those lessons that are full of doom, like last week's reading from Zephariah? "I will bring distress on men, so that they shall walk like the blind, because they have sinned against the Lord; their blood shall be poured out like dust, and their flesh like dung." Pause. "The word of the Lord," the reader says. Pause. We know our line, but it is hard to pronounce with feeling. But pronounce it we do, if not with feeling, then with pure, blind faith. "Thanks be to God," we say, because we believe that God is somewhere to be found in everything that happens to us. "Thanks be to God," we say, because we believe that the cords of God's love are never severed, however dark or convoluted our path through life may sometimes be.

God is God, and our lives are our lives, and we can love them or leave them, give thanks for them or whittle them away with regret. Our dare this morning is to embrace

47

all that we have ever been and done and haul it up to lay upon the altar, and there to recognize our lives as sacraments – as outward and visible signs of an inward and spiritual grace, with every single occurrence of our lives to be understood as an invitation to draw closer to God, to become part of his body, and therefore worthy of praise and blessing and thanksgiving.

So happy Thanksgiving. Happy Eucharist. Whether we leave this place to join friends and family or to dine alone, whether we look forward to a five course feast, three burgers at the Krystal or a free supper at the Union Mission, God goes with us and there is no corner of our lives that he does not inhabit. Let us be on the lookout for him, and ready with our chorus: "Thanks be to God. Alleluia. Amen."

ALL SAINTS
The Company of Heaven

After this I looked, and behold, a great multitude which no man could number, from every nation, from all tribes and peoples and tongues, standing before the throne and before the Lamb, clothed in white robes, with palm branches in their hands, and crying out with a loud voice, "Salvation belongs to our God who sits upon the throne, and to the Lamb!"
Revelation 7.9-10 RSV

This week has been a busy one on the church calendar – Thursday was All Saints' Day and Friday was the feast of All Souls. The distinction between the two is one we have all but lost, but in the old days it went like this: on All Saints' Day we remember all those saints who have left a name, whose stories we know something about, like Saint Peter, Saint Paul, or Saint Mary. Then on All Souls' Day we remember all the faithful departed, whether they made a mark in the world or not, the saints known to God alone, like our relatives, our friends, or the old woman across the street. Between the two we come into communion with all those saints and souls who have gone before us, with all our kin, known or unknown, to whom we are related by Christ's blood. This is "all the company of heaven" with whom we pray in celebrating the holy eucharist; this is "the communion of saints" about whom we sing.

Those of us who were here on Halloween night got a vivid illustration of that company, that communion. We gathered in the parish hall to celebrate All Hallow's Eve, to prepare ourselves for the feasts of All Saints and All Souls, and we came dressed as our favorite saints, or at least those were our instructions. John the Baptist was there – after his beheading, mind you, his head on a silver platter overflowing with fruit, with a cardboard box table hiding the rest of his alter-ego's body – and Saint Francis, with little stuffed birds sewn all over her, yes *her,* garment. Saint Cecelia was there, Saint Nicholas and Saint Louis – the city, that is, not the person – with a great silver arch above her head labeled "Gateway to the West."

Then there were those who had not read the instructions, or maybe they were just more enlightened in their understanding of sanctity – two cowboys, one of whom failed utterly to persuade the Cub Scouts that he was *not* Kenny Rogers, a mother and son pirate team, Garfield the cat, and not one but two Crayola crayons, one red and one blue, both crushed that someone else had the same idea. There was lots of hilarity and games and a loud parade before a panel of judges who chose the best costumes. After all the awards were passed out we were all given glittery halos to wear to church, beautiful little silvery things that hovered over our heads like the real things. Still a little giggly, we all marched over to the dimly lit sanctuary and took our places for the service, our halos bobbing and swaying and sparkling in the light of the candles. It was funny. It was eerie. It was like looking at a time exposure, with characters from all the centuries gathered around, appearing in us, becoming incarnate through us, our faces behind their own. What bound us all together, what all of us had in common, were those delicate, bobbing halos, linking us with each other and with all God's saints in all times and places.

How did we come by those halos? There are lots of answers from which to choose. According to Roman Catholic tradition there are two things necessary for sainthood: proof of a good and pious life, confirmed by evidence of at least three miracles after death – a little out of reach for most of us. Then there are the Beatitudes. It is no mistake that they are read every year on All Saints' Day: blessed are the poor in spirit, those who mourn, who are meek, peacemakers who are persecuted for righteousness' sake, for theirs is the kingdom of heaven. Who could compose a list of more saintly virtues, or a list of more impossible ones? Like the Ten Commandments, the Beatitudes confront us with an ideal vision – God's vision – of who we can be. But most of us read them like paragraphs of a job description and decide that it is futile even to apply. Our mistake when we do that, when we admit defeat before we ever start, is believing that sainthood is a carrot on a stick, something we must achieve, earn, arrive at, by self-sacrifice; that if we *do* the Ten Commandments, or *do* the Beatitudes, then we may finally *be* saints.

The reality is quite different. The reality is that, in our worship this morning, we witnessed the making of three new saints in the sacrament of holy baptism. The reality is that all of us who have been baptized are already saints, have already been given our halos, because all it takes to be a saint is to belong to God. It is not a matter of being or doing good or wearing a hair shirt or even of working three miracles that can be documented for the Vatican. It is simply a matter of joining up with the body of Christ, which is the source of all holiness and sanctity and blessedness. Once you have linked up with Christ's body, once you have been baptized in his name and shared his body and blood, you have everything you need to be a saint. You have your identity, your halo, and a choice: to live like who you are or not.

Now this is complicated, or maybe it only sounds complicated because such simple truths confound our ears, but the truth is that we are already saints. It is also true that God gives us the freedom to forsake this birthright, to fail to live up to it, to choose not to exercise the capacity for sainthood that belongs to all of us. It is like being a prisoner who has received a pardon, says theologian Karl Barth. You are a free person; your freedom is a reality, but until you get up and walk through the door of your cell you are a prisoner of your own failure to act. Or if you do not warm up to that analogy, try this one: it is like knowing there is a check for a million dollars in the next room with your name on it. The money is yours; you are a millionaire, but until you claim it and cash it you are as poor as if it were not there. Common sense puts it another way: use it or lose it, the saying goes, and that is the way it is with sainthood too. Once we have been baptized, once we have received our halos, we are saints. Our vocation, our calling from that point on, is to act like we are, to exercise our sainthood, to practice it, so that we do not lose our God-given capacity to be saints.

Do the Beatitudes sound any different in that light? I hope so. Each phrase deserves a sermon of its own, but read between the lines and this is what you hear: You are loved; act like it. You are redeemed; act like it. You are a saint; act like it. Become what you already are and you will be blessed with every breath you take, because blessedness, which means happiness, which means joy, which means fullness of life – blessedness is just what happens when you are who you were created to be, living the life you were created to live. Which is, incidentally, what the kingdom of God is all about.

So that is what we are up to today, recognizing our sainthood, remembering the saints who have gone before us and welcoming some new saints into the communion of all the saints. On this day especially we are all gathered together in one place, the old saints with their sickles and the baby saints in their diapers, passing one another on our ways in and out of this world. Can you feel what a crowd we are today? Mary and Joseph with their boy Jesus, the apostle Paul and Stephen the deacon, Origen and Julian of Norwich, Thomas Becket and Thomas More, Martin Luther King Jr. and Mother Teresa – angels and archangles and all the company of heaven, and every one of us by name – all sainted by God through the waters of baptism, all related by the blood of Christ, all of us with halos, whether we can see them or not, whether we are living up to them or not, bobbing and swaying and sparkling above our heads.

51

III.
THE INHABITANTS
OF
EARTH

DOUBT
Are You The One?

Now when John heard in prison about the deeds of the Christ, he sent word by his disciples and said to him, "Are you he who is to come, or shall we look for another?" And Jesus answered them, "Go and tell John what you hear and see: the blind receive their sight and the lame walk, lepers are cleansed and the deaf hear, and the dead are raised up, and the poor have good news preached to them. And blessed is he who takes no offense at me."
Matthew 11.2-6 RSV

Jesus is well into his career when this exchange takes place. The Sermon on the Mount is already history, as are the healings of the Gerasene demoniac, Jairus' daughter, and Peter's mother-in-law, among others. His ministry has taken root and the crowd of believers around him is growing, when out of their midst comes one plaintive, haunting chord of doubt: "Are you the one who is to come, or shall we look for another?" Who in the world wants to know, and where has he been that he needs to ask?

It is John speaking, through one of his own disciples, John the Baptizer, who recognized Jesus from his mother's womb, leaping with joy when her cousin Mary came to call. Wild-eyed John, who from his birth was called the prophet of the Most High, who lived in the desert alone, crying out when anyone approached, "Prepare the way of the Lord; clear a straight path for him." Stern John, who knew Jesus the moment he laid eyes on him at the river Jordan. "Do you come to me?" he said. "I need rather to be baptized by you." John, who was there when heaven opened and the spirit of God descended upon Jesus like a dove; John, who devoted his entire life to the coming Messiah. What has happened to him, that he should suddenly doubt Jesus' identity? "Are you the one who is to come, or shall we look for another?" Who can fathom the feeling behind that question? Anger, hurt, disappointment, fear: "*Are you the one?*"

Things were not going well for John, that was for certain. In the first place, he was in jail, a hellhole on the eastern shore of the Dead Sea. He was in trouble with Herod, and Salome would soon be asking for his head on a silver platter. Nothing was happening the way he had seen it. The Messiah was supposed to change things. He was supposed to fix it so that the wicked no longer prospered and the righteous, like himself, were saved. At one word from the Messiah the very walls of his prison should come tumbling down, but far from rescuing John, Jesus was into increasing trouble himself, and he showed no signs of living up to John's expectations. While John ate locusts in the wilderness, Jesus was changing water to wine at a wedding in Cana; while John crossed the street to avoid traffic with sinners, Jesus sought them out and invited himself home to eat with them; worst of all, while John had spent his whole life warning people to repent and save their souls, Jesus came along and told them to leave the saving to God, that what they were called to do was to love one another. Over and over John handed Jesus the ax, urging him to strike at the rotten wood of the world; over and over Jesus declined, pointing out the new growth, the green places that John could not or would not see. It not only confused John; it broke him. "Are you the one, or shall we look for another?"

It is not too hard to understand what John was going through. By simple virtue of sitting where we do this morning we make the statement that we, like John, have recognized the Messiah in Jesus. We are all, in our different ways, preparing the way of the Lord. Every week, right here, we recite the creed and confess that Christ is Lord and every week we search for new, more effective ways to teach and preach and live that truth. Along the way, we have acquired some definite ideas about our Lord; as students of the Bible, of tradition, and of our own experience, we have certain expectations of him and what he will, sooner or later, do for us his people. But who is innocent of doubt? Who has never – in anger, hurt, disappointment, loss – who has never asked John's question? *Jesus, are you the one, or shall we look for another?*

You are, for instance, watching the evening news, which begins with some new bombing in the Middle East. Broken soldiers on stretchers, fresh outrage from the officials, the president calls another news conference. At home, there are trucks full of sand bags in the nation's capital, a blizzard in the midwest, old people freezing to death under their thin quilts. Across town, the most recent murder, more grisly than the last; another child beaten and abandoned, a fire that burns everything one struggling family owns. You do not make it to the sports or weather; you turn off the set, sit in the darkness and wonder, *Jesus, are you the one, or shall we look for another?*

Or you are visiting a couple in the hospital, really lovely people who have been married for eleven years and who have been trying to have a child for ten of those. After almost a decade of tests, of drugs and surgical procedures, they conceived, and their joy knew no bounds. They did everything right. She ate only the purest foods, he learned how to deliver the baby himself, and all signs were go. Until her labor began, anyhow, and went on and on – twelve hours, then twenty four, then thirty. The doctors begged her to let them help and when she was too weak to argue she let them. Moments later they handed her a boy, her firstborn, whom she now holds out to you. You look at his almond-shaped eyes and cannot mistake the signs – he has Down's syndrome, sure enough – but neither can you mistake the love on his parents' faces, love and grief, and complete bewilderment. You kiss the child, hand him back, and think, *Jesus, are you the one, or shall we look for another?*

Or you answer the buzzer at the church door again and again, opening it to poor people in such numbers that they begin to look alike to you: dirty, wrinkled, bloodshot, unshaven, ashamed. You begin to hate them for needing more than you have to give. There have been five of them today. One needs glasses, two a ride to the Farmer's Market where they hope to find work; one needs an apartment, and the last a costly operation. All of them are desperate for money and food. Two of them, admittedly drunk but genuinely hungry, accept cold sausages and biscuits from the kitchen and, while your back is turned, take three cans of Sterno as well. You hope they are planning to heat the sausages with the stuff and not to drink it. You show them the door and think, *Jesus, are you the one, or shall we look for another?*

With Isaiah, with John, you want to rail, "Be strong! Fear not! Behold, your God will come with a vengeance, with the recompense of God. He will come and save you!" But it does not seem to happen that way, at least not yet. Over and over we hand Jesus the ax and he lays it down again, sending us back into the desert, into the city, into our lives, with words of love on our lips – to help carry a load of grief, to steady a shaking hand, to pass out a few cold sausages and biscuits. They seem puny efforts, these pantomimes of love, and they do not often satisfy, not the way a little vengeance would, a God with an ax. But they are the tasks we have been given to do, and we have promised to try. It is, perhaps, a matter of serving the God who *is* instead of the one we would have him be – something that was hard for poor disillusioned John; something that is not much easier for us today.

"Are you the one who is to come, or shall we look for another?" And Jesus answered them, "Go tell John what you hear and see: the blind receive their sight and the lame walk, lepers are cleansed and the deaf hear, and the dead are raised up, and the poor have good news preached to them. And blessed is he who takes no offense at me." It is a radical answer, almost as radical as the question, an answer delivered completely in the passive voice, without a single claim for the speaker. There are no "I" statements here – the blind are seeing and the lame are walking, but who is responsible? Jesus refuses, apparently, to take charge, to take credit, to drop his humanity as if it were a disguise and singlehandedly rescue the human race from the circumstances of their lives. Put on the spot, asked point blank to prove himself, he gives his power away. "Go and tell John what *you* hear and see," he says, however much we wish he would work a showy miracle on the spot. Open your eyes, he says, see for yourself, make up your own minds. Or, in the words of the psalmist, "Taste and see that the Lord is good."

"And blessed is he who takes no offense at me," he concludes, in one of the most ignored passages of all time. The Greek word for offense is *skandalon,* which makes the literal translation something more like, "And blessed is he who is not scandalized by me." But what the word meant to the ancient Greeks was a stumbling block, so that the best translation is "And blessed is he who does not get tripped up on me." What is Jesus saying? That the Messiah has not come to be the center of attention? That he has not come to ascend a throne, to fulfill all the expectations of his people? It sounds that way. It sounds as if he has come not to wield power but to give it away, to be himself, to glorify God, and finally to disappear into the crowd of those who have found his love contagious.

What is Jesus saying? It sounds as if he is saying, "Go tell John that everyone who is expected has already arrived; go tell him what you hear and see – that things may not be working out the way he wanted them to but that every now and then, in surprising places, marvelous things are happening. People who were blind to the love loose in the world have received their sight; people who were paralyzed with fear are limber with hope; people who were deaf from want of good news are singing hymns. And best and most miraculous of all, tell John that this is not the work of one lonely Messiah but the work of God, carried out by all who believe, and that there is no end in sight. Tell him I am the one, if you must, but tell him also that *yes* he should look for another, and another, and another. Tell him to search every face for the face of God and not to get tripped up on me, because what is happening here is bigger than any of us; what is coming to pass is as big as the Kingdom of God."

There is a tradition, among the Jews who celebrate Passover, of saving a seat at their Seder feast for Elijah, the prophet who is supposed to bring the news that the Messiah has finally come. At a poignant moment in the service, the door is flung open for Elijah and everyone falls silent with anticipation. For thousands of years that door has been opened, and for thousands of years all that has entered has been the wind. One Hasidic story tells of a pious Jew who asked his rabbi, "For about forty years I have opened the door for Elijah every Seder night waiting for him to come, but he never does. What is the reason?" The rabbi answered, "In your neighborhood there lives a very poor family with many children. Call on the man and propose to him that you and your family celebrate the next Passover at his house, and for this purpose provide him and his whole family with everything necessary for the eight days of Passover. Then on the Seder night Elijah will certainly come."

The man did as the rabbi told him, but after Passover he came back and claimed that again he had waited in vain to see Elijah. The rabbi answered, "I know very well that Elijah came on the Seder night to the house of your poor neighbor. But of course you could not see him." And the rabbi held a mirror before the face of the man and said, "Look, this was Elijah's face that night."

SERVICE
Local Miracles

"How many loaves have you?" he asked; "go and see." They found out and told him, "Five, and two fishes also." He ordered them to make the people sit down in groups on the green grass, and they sat down in rows, a hundred rows of fifty each. Then, taking the five loaves and the two fishes, he looked up to heaven, said the blessing, broke the loaves, and gave them to the disciples to distribute. He also divided the two fishes among them. They all ate to their hearts' content; and twelve great basketfuls of scraps were picked up, and what was left of the fish. Those who ate the loaves numbered five thousand men.

Mark 6.38-44 NEB

This story – about how five thousand people sat down and ate their fill on five barley buns and two fishes – is the only miracle story agreed up on by all four of the gospel writers. The raising of Lazarus, for instance, appears only in John; the healing of the blind man of Bethsaida is found only in Mark; the healing of the ten lepers only in Luke. But the feeding of the five thousand appears in all four gospels, which means not only that it was a very important story for the early church, but also that it probably happened much the way we hear it today.

But that is not saying too much, given our modern powers of interpretation. One such interpretation is that the meal was symbolic, that the five thousand pinched off tiny, tiny pieces of fish and bread so that there was enough to go around. But what about the twelve baskets of leftovers? Well, in that case the interpretation is that just about all of the five thousand had a little supper tucked away in their tunics, a little something to sneak off and eat by themselves – but that when they saw how freely the disciples offered to share what they had, they all pulled their own meals out of hiding and passed everything around. And then, of course, there is the third possibility: that it was a miracle, that Jesus took five loaves and two fishes and by the grace of God used them to cater a dinner on the lawn for five thousand. So those are three of the possibilities, and there is no one to say which we should believe. For all the questions it raises, the Bible is not a book with the answers in the back, but as a rule the answers we choose tell us something about our faith.

To go back to the faith of the early church, this story was important not least of all because it foreshadowed God's big banquet for his chosen people at the end of time. That great feast gets talked about a lot in the Bible, and Jesus gave us a continuing reminder of it in the sacrament of his body and blood. His actions at that last supper were the same as his actions in this story: he took the bread, blessed it, broke it, and gave it. So as twentieth century Christians we tend to look upon the feeding of the five thousand as a sort of eucharist, and that makes it hard to remember that the people who actually were there did not see it that way at all. They knew little of Jesus' significance, and nothing of his death and resurrection, and certainly nothing about a holy meal of bread and wine that would change the face of history. They were just hungry – for food, for health, for understanding – and this man Jesus seemed committed to feeding them.

What they *did* know were some of the old stories about how God Almighty fed his people in various miraculous ways, sending manna to sustain Israel in the wilderness, sending ravens to feed the prophet Elijah with bread and meat. In the second book of Kings there is a story very much like today's, about how the prophet Elisha fed a hundred soldiers with twenty barley loaves and a few ears of corn. In every case, the situation looked hopeless, the people despaired, and God provided. So the crowd was hopeful. Rumor had it that Jesus, like Moses and Elijah and Elisha before him, was a man of God. They watched him, followed him, pushed their way to the front of the crowd, reached out their hands to him, implored him. And he healed many of them, but on this particular day he is weary and discouraged. He has been separated from his disciples for some time. They have just returned from traveling two by two through the countryside and have brought back with them the grim news of John the Baptist's death, a totally unnecessary death at the whim of a dancing girl. Jesus wants some time alone with them to absorb the news, wants some time to himself. "Come away by yourselves to a lonely place," he tells them, "and rest a while."

So they do, climbing into a boat together and sailing downshore a ways, hoping to escape the crowd. But the crowd is hungry, and hunger does not easily give up the prospect of food. So the crowd follow, picking their way along the shore of the lake, some of them keeping an eye on the boat while others run to get their friends. The end result is that when Jesus and his disciples moor their boat they step into the midst of the same crowd they had hoped to leave behind. It is not hard to imagine several realistic responses to such a situation: Jesus could turn his back and stay in the boat to catch up with his disciples, or could even sail on, for that matter. He could scold the crowd for following him and ask them to disperse, telling them he has no more to offer them this day. Or he could throw an uncharacteristic temper tantrum, reminding them that he is just one, single person, as much in need of a little rest as the next guy and fed up with their demands. But he chooses none of those. With every reason in the world to choose anger, resentment, or despair, he chooses compassion. He looks at the crowd and through some holy optical illusion sees not a crowd but a collection of people – a woman with a frail baby in her arms, a gaunt man with a withered hand, a boy with a face full of questions about the meaning of his life. He sees all these *people,* like sheep without a shepherd, and he lays aside his own need in favor of theirs. He may not have much to offer them just now, but what he has he gives, teaching them all afternoon.

When it grows late his disciples – whom we may imagine are a little less compassionate than their friend – point out to Jesus, as if he did not already know, that the sun is going down and there is no food in sight. "Send them away," they suggest, wanting someone else to solve the problem, but Jesus has a better idea. "You give them something to eat," he says, and the problem boomerangs back into their shins. It is hopeless, can't he see that? There is no money, no food, not even a house in sight, and we are talking *five thousand people* here. Even if the disciples gave all they had, it would not make a dent in the hunger of the crowd. It would be a waste of their meager resources. Let someone who has more do it: better yet, let the people take care of themselves. And Jesus says to them, "How many loaves *do* you have?" They do not know for sure what they have; they just know it is not enough, that they do not have what it takes to meet the challenge. And Jesus says, "Go and see."

If we have not already stepped into this story, here is our opening. Is there anyone who does not know what it is like to face a hungry crowd, a hungry world, with five loaves and two fishes? Hundreds of homeless women and children competing for fifty spaces on the floor at the YWCA: there is not enough to go around, Lord. Whole nations perishing for lack of food: everything we have would not help, Lord. A national budget so in debt and out of whack it seems doomed: there is nothing we can do, Lord. It is too big. We are too small. Send them away. Do not ask us. We have not got enough to go around. And he said to them, "How many loaves *do* you have? Go and see."

Over the last couple of weeks I have had the dubious honor of driving to Arizona and back with nine teenagers and my infinitely good-natured spouse. We went to repair homes on a Navajo Indian reservation. We went with half a dozen paint brushes and some other assorted tools, most of us with only a vague notion of how to paint a house or build a flight of steps. We went, in other words, with something less than five loaves and two fishes, and the Navajos knew it. The tribal officials who had approved our visit had been told repeatedly that 240 teenagers would arrive on July 7, but when we got there very few arrangements had been made. It turned out that they did not believe we were really coming, so they did not buy their share of the supplies. Anglos had made promises to them before, they said, and nothing had come of it. So they had waited to see, and what they saw two Sunday afternoons ago were 240 kids from Vermont, from Minnesota, from California, Texas and Georgia getting out of vans and buses and cars – getting out in their cut-offs, with their bedrolls and water pistols, with piles of empty soft drink cans and bubble gum wrappers cascading out the doors behind them. Needless to say, there were not many engineers, electricians, plumbers or contractors among them – just a crowd of sleepy, skinny, confused-looking kids.

There was a steady stream of traffic by the Window Rock Unified School that afternoon, Navajos in cars, on bicycles, on foot, cruising by to check out the scene, and I imagine there were some pretty good laughs around their dinner tables that night. "Did you see who they sent to work on our houses? A bunch of kids!" That is, at least, what many of us were thinking about ourselves. Five crummy loaves and two little dried up fishes. The next morning we were sent out in work groups of five to some forty homes, many as far as thirty miles away, with instructions to build a sheep pen, roof a house, build a porch. My own group was handed eight boxes of linoleum tile, some scrapers, glue, razor blades, a measuring tape, a couple of doors and an electric drill. I was delighted with it all but had absolutely no idea how it all went together, nor did any of my crew. The drill provided us all with a good laugh, at least, since Frank and Dolly Hart's three room house had neither electricity nor running water. We had no idea what to do, so we just started doing it. The Navajos were amazed by our industry, and we had lots of visitors who came by just to watch us work.

Two days into the week my infinitely good-natured spouse said he was feeling a little discouraged, that he was having a hard time understanding why we had driven 1700 miles just to paint someone's bedroom. Five crummy loaves and two little dried up fishes. He wanted to be doing something important, like building a hospital or working on a school. I heard similar comments from other workers – their project was so small, there was so much more that needed to be done, their efforts would not make a dent in the Navajos' sixteen million acres of need.

Then halfway through the week a funny thing began to happen. Navajos who had been watching us from the sidelines began to pitch in. Old Mr. Hart, who could not walk without a cane, patched the sheetrock in the room where we were working. Larry Silversmith worked all day long on his grandmother's house with another crew and then continued long after they left each night, finishing up whatever they had left undone. At a third work site, a whole crowd of young Navajos showed up to help rebuild Annie Begay's hogan (the traditional log and earth dwelling in which many Navajos live). If a bunch of Anglo kids would come all the way from Vermont to work on old Annie's house, they said, they guessed the least they could do was help. There were so many of them that they almost put our teenagers out of business, but Annie said to let them work, that it was a miracle. She said she had been praying for the day those boys would wake up from their sleep and do something for someone else. She said it was an answer to her prayers. Five crummy loaves and two little dried up fishes.

At the end of the week, forty-two out of the week's forty-six projects were complete. Thousands of dollars had been spent as well as something in the neighborhood of 5500 work hours. The reservation was dotted with new roofs, new paint, new corrals, new tile, new stucco, new porches. A representative from the Navajo youth organization stood up to thank us. She gave the director of the work camp two Navajo rugs, several portraits of their leaders, a huge Navajo Nation flag and 240 smaller ones for each of us to take home. She said that made us honorary Navajos. She said they would never doubt us again, and when we came back they would be ready for us. And finally, through her tears, she said they loved us and would never forget us.

Do I need to say it more directly? We went into the week skinny, with five loaves and two fishes, but we came out fat, with twelve baskets to spare. Not because we did anything right; not because we had enough to give, but because God made good on his promise to match our gifts, such as they were, with his own. It is something to remember, when the crowd looks too big, the odds too poor, the work too hard, the situation too hopeless. It is something to remember when our own resources look too meager, our efforts too puny, our spirits too low.

Stop staring at the crowd; go look at your loaves. How many do you have? Any answer will do. Now follow the leader; *take* what you have – whatever you have got, take it into your hands and hold it lightly, very lightly; then *bless* it – thank God for what you have got and make it holy by giving it away for love; then *break* it – sorry, but you have to tear it up to share it – no way to keep it all in one nice piece; and finally *give* it – to whoever is standing in front of you, beside you – spread it around, and never mind that there does not seem to be enough for everyone. It is not up to you to feed the whole crowd, to solve the whole problem, to fix the whole world. It is just up to you to share what you have got, to feed whatever big or little hunger that happens to be standing right in front of you. The rest will come. Because God is God, the rest will come. For now, for your part, how many loaves *do* you have? Go and see.

PRAYER
After Words

Likewise the Spirit helps us in our weakness; for we do not know how to pray as we ought, but the Spirit himself intercedes for us with sighs too deep for words.

Romans 8.26 RSV

In the ancient oriental world, the employees of a king's court usually included at least one dignitary whose job it was to usher visitors into the presence of the royal highness. Anyone who wanted to see the king, whether to bring gifts from a neighboring kingdom, to beg mercy on behalf of a relative in trouble, or just to say hello – that person had to seek the goodwill of the doorkeeper or he never would lay eyes on the king. He did whatever he had to do to convince the doorkeeper of his sincerity; he flattered, cajoled, pleaded or reasoned with him, but if he succeeded, his reward was great. The doorkeeper would vouch for his genuineness and good intentions and he would have free access to the king forever after that.

Saint Paul's very good news is that we have not one but two such intercessors in the kingdom of God: the Holy Spirit, who teaches us how to pray, and Christ himself, who sits on the right hand of God. When we seek God's presence, Paul says, both of them stand ready to assure the ruler of the universe of our sincerity and good intentions. It is awesome good news, to have two advocates of such magnificence, but most of us do not take full advantage of them. It is because we do not know how to pray, Paul says. We do not know how, or what, or why, and consequently we are likely to avoid prayer altogether because we would rather not pray at all than do it wrong. God already knows what we ask before we ask it, right? And he knows better than we what we need, right? Half the things on our prayer list seems too trivial to bring up and the rest too weighty. We do not want to test God; we do not want to manipulate him, even if we could, and so we tie ourselves in knots before we ever begin, and we may put off beginning. We may in fact choose to remain silent before God rather than assault his majesty with our babble. It is an understandable idea – humble, and all that – but it is a little like refusing to make any friends because you are not sure what to say to them.

Talking is only part of prayer. We talk to unburden our hearts, to come clean before God; we talk to hear ourselves talk, to listen to how we present ourselves to our Maker, and quite often our prayers change even as we pray them. We realize we do not want what we thought we wanted. It occurs to us to pray for something else altogether. Or we pray for someone we do not even like. These changes are evidence of the Holy Spirit at work, Paul says, teaching us how to pray. But it is when we finish talking that our prayers begin in earnest, because that is when we begin to listen. When all of our words run out, when we are scraping the bottom of our verbal barrels and all that is left are some inarticulate longings, some hungers beyond expression, that is when the Holy Spirit really gets to work, bearing those pieces of our souls to God in a way that makes divine sense and returning to us with good news that may be equally inarticulate, equally beyond expression. But if we are listening we cannot fail to hear it, and be changed by it, and reassured that even when we do not know how to pray our prayers make their way to God, ushered into his presence by the two best advocates the world has ever known.

I knew more about this when I was in seminary than I do now, perhaps because I was so new to it, and had fewer words to distract me. My first semester in New Haven was an extremely difficult one. There were no catastrophic events to speak of, but I was further away from home than I had ever been, and everyone seemed to speak a foreign language, and I was not even sure why I was there. I was dreadfully lonely, and afraid, and desperate for some answers. Next door to the divinity school, on the highest hill in town, stood an old deserted Victorian mansion. The sagging porch was overcome with weeds, the slate shingles were crumbling off the roof, and all the doors and windows were boarded up. A metal fire escape ran up one side for a full three stories and ended in a little metal platform outside an attic dormer window. The whole place was plastered with "No Trespassing" signs and the campus police patrolled it regularly.

But one night, at the end of my rope, I decided that maybe if I braved all my fears – including a considerable fear of heights – and climbed up there to the top, I would be able to pray a prayer that would win an answer. So I did, one shaky step at a time, and arrived at the top with my heart in my throat. It was extraordinarily beautiful up there. I could see all the way to the Long Island Sound, where the nearly full moon made glitter out of the water, and through all the treetops in between I could see street lights and shop lights and porch lights winking through the leaves. There was a strong wind off the sound, a salty wind, that gusted through the eaves of the old house and made it creak.

Once the edge of my fear was gone, I began my prayer, asking God to reveal his purpose for me, to point me in the right direction, to give me a sign. It was a pretty good prayer, as formal prayers go, but I did not hear or feel any answers. So I tried again, getting madder and madder as I did. What good was God, if he would not even answer a simple prayer? I talked and talked at him, until the words ran out, and then to my great surprise I heard myself begin to sing – or chant, really, something between plainsong and the howl of a dog answering a siren. No words came out, just mournful sounds that seemed finally to say what was on my heart, and when I came to the end of them I had my answer. It was nothing specific, which was what I wanted. I wanted a fortune cookie answer, like "Take the next boat to Samoa and dig latrines in Pago-Pago." But the answer I got was the deep conviction that I was loved, and that what I was called to do was to love back, in whatever way allowed me to love the best and most – as a housewife and mother, as a nuclear physicist, a gas station attendant, an ordained minister – the specifics did not seem to matter to God. What mattered were my relationships, and the love in them, chief among which was my relationship with God. Saint Augustine summed it up 1500 years ago: "Love and do what you will."

But that sort of answer does not sit well with most of us. It is a frightening world out there, with a thousand possibilities for doing good or evil, and we want more certainty than that. We want the definitive word; we want specific instructions; we want clear guidelines for what is acceptable and what is unacceptable behavior before God. We want to be rescued from our freedom, and we burn rubber seeking a simplicity that simply does not exist. The vehicle most of us use in this search is the Bible. I have been surprised by how many people have come to ask me what the Bible says about this romantic predicament or that job offer or their quarrel with a friend. Some of them want to know if they should let the Bible fall open at will or close their eyes and point to a passage for the answer to their question, which reminds me a little of reading tea leaves or consulting the I-Ching.

Let me hasten to add that the motives of these people are entirely honorable – they are seeking the will of God for their lives – but what is surprising is that they are so often willing to put the answers they find in the Bible on a pedestal above the answers they find in their own minds and hearts, in the counsel of their friends, and in the world around them. To do so seems tantamount to saying that the Holy Spirit has ceased to function, that God can only speak to us in the word he used thousands of years ago, and that there is nothing new under the sun. Before I go further, let me reaffirm the vow that all priests make at their ordinations: I do believe the Holy Scriptures of the Old and New Testaments to be the Word of God, and to contain all things necessary for salvation. That is true. It is true because, in addition to lots of laws, a few tedious genealogies and some sound advice, what the Bible contains are lots of biographies – the stories of Abraham and Sarah's relationship with God, Moses and Aaron and Miriam's relationship with God, Hosea and Habakkuk's, John the Baptist's, Mary and Joseph's, Peter's, Mary Magdalene's, Nicodemus', Judas' – it contains the stories all their relationships with God, and how he had particular things to say to each of them, how he loved each of them as his individual creations and not as recruits in some faceless army.

What all those stories tell us is that God's word, God's will for their lives, did not come to them in a printed manual, with specific answers to be found on page 536, paragraph 5, line 14. His will for them, which was his love for them, came in the form of a living relationship with them, which they were free to embrace or flee. What all of their stories combine to tell us – what the Bible tells us – is that God comes to us in the same way, that he calls each of us into relationship with him, and while searching scripture may be the way we come to understand that, it may also be the way we miss the boat altogether.

Certainly we can learn from all those stories, from the relationships God had with each of our mothers and fathers in the faith. But reading about their relationships cannot be a substitute for seeking our own. We are called to live out our own stories, to search for the unique shape our own lives will take in communion with God, and find his particular word to us. What does that mean, day to day? It means revering the Bible as the inspired word of God; but it also means revering the Christian tradition as the place that word has been hammered into action, and it means revering our own reason and intuition as God's best gifts to us, and revering our own experience as the arena in which God is working his purpose out through the activity of the Holy Spirit. It means searching in all those places for guidance about how and what and why to pray as we grow in our own relationship with God.

There are not many certainties in that prescription. We will probably never stop wanting them, but certainties do not have much to do with freedom, or love, or prayer – especially prayer. If we want to give up second-hand religion, religion we know about only through the Bible; if we want to shoot for our own living experience of the faith, we will spend an enormous amount of time in prayer, not only talking to God but listening to him, and listening sometimes to what sounds only like silence, or to our own wild howls and shuddering sighs, believing that the Holy Spirit groans with us, and bears what we cannot say to the throne of God, and there with Christ Jesus makes our prayers acceptable. Believing that, there is no prayer we cannot pray, and nothing in the silence to fear, and everything to gain. For "we know that in everything God works for good with those who love him, who are called according to his purpose." What is that purpose, for each of us? Ask. Pray. And listen – above all, listen.

FAITH
The Automatic Earth

He said, 'The kingdom of God is like this. A man scatters seed on the land; he goes to bed at night and gets up in the morning, and the seed sprouts and grows – how, he does not know. The ground produces a crop by itself, first the blade, then the ear, then full grown corn in the ear.'

Mark 4.26-28 NEB

At my house there is a gardener and there is a worrier. The gardener is a pretty easy-going fellow. Every May or June he comes through the door with a brown paper sack full of seed packets and a couple of evenings later he can be found puttering around the yard, emptying the packages into shallow furrows, heaping the dirt into little mounds and curling pieces of fence around them to keep the dogs out. Several weeks later, plants appear in the strangest places. He has been known to plant green peppers between the azalea bushes and broccoli by the mailbox. For the second year in a row there is a stand of asparagus pushing up through the roots of the crepe myrtle tree and sweet pea vines winding through the branches of the weeping cherry. In a few weeks, string beans will overtake the back deck of the house, covering everything in sight like kudzu.

All of this drives the worrier crazy. She knows how gardens are supposed to be and *this is not it*. You are supposed to begin by buying a book, for one thing, with illustrations on how to arrange plants according to size, height, and drainage requirements. Everything goes in straight rows. First you must test the soil; then you must fertilize, you must mulch, must weed, must water; you must above all *worry* or else how will your garden grow? To her eternal dismay and amazement, there comes one day every summer when the gardener proclaims that the vegetables are ready. He goes out to collect them from all over the burgeoning yard and a little while later the worrier sits down to a table heaped with manna. Against her will and better judgment she has to admit that he has done all right, in spite of his refusal to worry. This year there are even two dill plants that appeared out of nowhere, gifts from the earth itself.

This is what the kingdom of God is like, according to Mark. A man scatters seed on the ground and goes about his business, trusting the seed to sprout without his further interference, because the ground produces of itself, first the blade, then the ear, then the full grain in the ear. The Greek here is wonderful: the ground is, literally, *automatic*. It produces of itself; it has within itself the power to make a seed become a plant, and so the kingdom of God is likened to automatic earth, earth that can be trusted to yield its fruit without any cheerleading, any manure, any worry on our part. The seed sprouts and grows, we know not how. Call it agricultural grace.

All right then; I will not worry any more about my string beans and squash – the automatic earth can be trusted – but what about my life? There is nothing automatic about that. If I do not attend to it, manage it and yes, worry about it, I will fail, fail at what I want to do, be found wanting at the end, die unsatisfied and unnoticed. Help! Saint Paul is right; in this earthly tent I do groan, do sigh with anxiety, but not exactly for the reasons he says. When I first read today's passage from second Corinthians out loud, I began by nodding my head a lot. "We know," Paul says, "that if the earthly tent we live in is destroyed we have a building from God." *Well yes, we hope that. Cannot be too presumptuous, after all, cannot really know, but yes, a building to replace this tent sounds heavenly.* "Here indeed we groan." *Do we ever groan; yessirree, he is right about that, and anxiety –* "We sigh with anxiety" *– what a mind reader; that is exactly what we do –* "So that what is mortal may be swallowed up by life" *– what a beautiful phrase, swallowed up by life.* "So we are always of good courage" *– well, we try; we may not always be courageous but we are brave from time to time –* "and we would rather be away from the body and at home with the Lord." *What was that? Actually, we sort of like it here in the body, all things considered. There is no particular hurry to leave,* *is there?* "For we must all appear before the judgment seat of Christ." *Oh groan, here comes the anxiety again –*

Paul names the big worries, death and judgment, but fill in your own variations: nuclear war, cancer, poverty, divorce, addiction, pollution. What is it that makes your heart chatter in your chest? What feeds your ulcer, makes your shoulder cramp, keeps you awake at night? Where are you busiest protecting yourself and those you love, where does it seem like there is ultimately no hope, where is it in particular that you do not quite trust God to be God? Someone says, "Have faith!" and you want to break something, want to shout, "Faith is not enough!"

We live in an age of anxiety. To go back to the agricultural metaphor, we live between the time of planting and the harvest, and it is a time of great uncertainty. We want to trust the automatic earth; we want to believe that what God has begun he will bring to fruition, but just in case he does not we hedge our bets, doing everything we can think of to keep the anxiety at bay. Sometimes we call what we are doing "helping God out." Sure we can trust him with our lives, but just to help him along we frequent the health food shop, the investment broker, the insurance agent, maybe even duck into the astrologer's storefront on Euclid Avenue to have our palms read – just for fun – to see what is ahead. Anything to batten down the hatches, to make the future look a little more secure.

But that is only one symptom of anxiety. There are lots more. Like *perfectionism* – the need to do everything exactly right, according to the book, so that there can be no doubt about our superiority. Or *drivenness* – that compulsion that turns all our "want to's" into "have to's," that raises our demands on ourselves and others to a fever pitch. There is *moral outrage* – our insistence that we who have worked so hard have earned the right to be protected from all harm; bad things should not happen to good people. Or how about *restlessness* – the swinging foot, the tapping finger, the vague unease that says we should never be where we are but somewhere else instead; cannot sleep, cannot sit still for long; got to keep moving, got to stay busy. Then there is *the dread of being alone* – faced with the prospect of a night at home by ourselves, we get on the telephone and see what we can rustle up, or, failing that, settle into five or six hours of fellowship with the television set or video machine. Along with that estrangement from self comes *estrangement from God* – we buy books on spirituality but read mysteries instead; we mean to pray but it is hard to find the time and when we do we fall asleep. Sometimes it just seems like there is nobody there.

The word is anxiety – *angst* in German – a straight or narrow passage such as to restrict breathing; uneasiness or trouble of mind about some uncertain event, like my life, my death, my relationship with God. Anxiety is so much a part of modern life that *it* seems automatic, an occupational hazard of being a finite creature in a universe of infinite possibilities. But anxiety is more than that, more than just a quirk of my creatureliness to be taken for granted. Insofar as my anxiety keeps me separated from God, from other human beings and from my own soul, I am prepared to call anxiety a sin, and one that calls for my repentance, because it keeps me in limbo, telling me on one hand that I must work out my own salvation and on the other that I am doomed to fail. In short, what is absent when anxiety is present is faith – faith that God will be God, that the automatic earth will yield its fruit, that life can be trusted.

I am not, of course, advocating that we all lie down under the nearest fig tree and watch the clouds go by, although that might not be a bad idea for most of us. Giving up anxiety does not mean giving up responsibility, or concern, or the wish to live a productive life. But is does mean giving up our incessant, sterile worrying about what will become of us and our poisonous illusion that if we do stop worrying our lives will collapse. This is sin, and the remedy for it is twofold: first confession, and then, amendment of life. Do you desire to be saved from the sin of anxiety? Then get on your knees and confess it – confess everything you have tried to control, all the ways you have tried to manufacture your own security, all the times you have turned away from God in order to seek your own solutions. Confess what it has cost you, and how poorly it has worked to bring you peace. Then ask for forgiveness, the forgiveness that is yours before you ask, and within the freedom of that forgiveness amend your life. Make a different choice, a choice against anxiety, and live out of that choice for a change.

Saint Paul's word is as good as any: choose *courage,* which is not the absence of fear but the willingness to go on in spite of it. Choose to face your life, your death, your God, the dangerous unknown – just choose to face it without resorting to the old perfectionism, the old drivenness, the old restlessness and outrage. Choose courage, even knowing as you do that you cannot choose it once and for all, that if it is what you want you must choose it over and over again, every day that you live, if real living is what you are after. That is what it takes. Confession and choice, forgiveness and courage, over and over, a new way of life.

Then scatter your seeds. Anxiety would have you keep them in your pocket, or plant them in small pots, or dig them up every day to see if they are growing. Courage allows you to open your hand and let them fly. They land where they land, and a few feed the birds, but many more fall into the ground and there in the dark, where you cannot see and do not know how, the automatic earth turns their death into life, pushing up through layers of dirt – through asphalt, through concrete if necessary, through whatever is in their way – first the blade, then the ear, then the full grain in the ear. Then it is your turn, you who have watched and waited faithfully, knowing you cannot make the seed grow, knowing who can – it is your turn to harvest the crop, and let your table be heaped with good things, and sit down at it, and eat.

DEATH
Without a Net

Then Mary, when she came where Jesus was and saw him, fell at his feet, saying to him, "Lord, if you had been here, my brother would not have died." When Jesus saw her weeping, and the Jews who came with her also weeping, he was deeply moved in spirit and troubled; and he said, "Where have you laid him?" They said to him, "Lord, come and see." Jesus wept. So the Jews said, "See how he loved him!" But some of them said, "Could not he who opened the eyes of the blind man have kept this man from dying?"

John 11.32-37 RSV

The story we have just heard about the raising of Lazarus is found only in the gospel according to John, and it is a disturbing story. In the first place, it seems that Lazarus' death was untimely. He was a contemporary of Jesus', along with his sisters Martha and Mary, which means that he was a young man – in his thirties, say, when he was felled by a mysterious illness. We are told that Jesus loved the whole family, and yet when he received word that Lazarus was ill, he did not drop everything and rush to his friend's side. Lazarus lived in Judea, for one thing, and Jesus was already in deep trouble with the authorities there. If he returned, he was likely to be arrested. But beyond that, the message was not an urgent one. "Sir, you should know that your friend lies ill," read the note from Martha and Mary. No reason for Jesus to believe that the illness was life-threatening, no warning that he should hurry.

For whatever reasons, he arrived in Bethany two days later to find that his friend Lazarus *had* died, and had been lying in his tomb for four days. According to Jewish custom, this meant that Lazarus' body had begun to rot and that his soul had departed; Jesus' friend was, in other words completely, irrevocably, dead. Without knowing that they did so, both Martha and Mary greeted Jesus with the same words, "Sir, if you had been here, my brother would not have died." There was no accusation in their words, no bitterness – the death was sudden, unexpected, tragic, but the women did not blame Jesus – they simply recognized that if he had been with Lazarus things would have turned out differently. But he was not, and Lazarus had been dead four days, and there was a lot of weeping on the part of those who were not ready to let him go.

Jesus' own response was puzzling. He was "deeply moved," the Bible says, but the word in Greek means more than that. It suggests that he was not only moved but angry, full of righteous wrath and ready to explode. Angry? At whom? The commentaries say he was angry because everyone was crying, which means that they had no faith in him, but that cannot be the whole story, because in the next moment he too was weeping. Jesus wept, and it is my wild and subjective guess that his tears were for the whole world, tears so full of anger and sadness that it was hard to tell where one left off and the other began: tears for his friends Martha and Mary in their grief; tears over the loss of his friend Lazarus; tears about the frailty of life and the randomness with which it was snuffed out; tears that no one seemed to understand what he was about, much less believe it; tears over the enormity of what he had been given to do, and how alone he was.

Jesus wept, and then he let Martha and Mary lead him to Lazarus' tomb. The text is factual here; we have no details to aid our imaginations, but who knows how an eyewitness might have described the scene? *At first he just stood there staring at the stone that blocked the mouth of the cave where Lazarus lay. He stared so that you would not have wanted to walk between him and that stone; he stared so that you would not have wanted him to look at you at all. Then he began to tremble, his whole body shaking with some great effort going on inside of him. His face grew dark, the veins in his neck stood out like ropes, and that is when the air started to crackle, just before he opened his mouth and bellowed like a bull, "Lazarus, come forth." Then there was a commotion in the earth, the sound of a thousand wings in the sky, and a moan from inside that tomb like someone being torn limb from limb. I tell you, if you had asked me who I would rather have faced at that moment, Lazarus or a Philistine coming at me with a sword, I would have chosen the Philistine.*

But is was Lazarus who came forth, stumbling out of his tomb wrapped in linen bandages, his face concealed by a cloth. "Loose him," Jesus said, "Let him go." And that is all we know about Lazarus. Yanked from the jaws of death, the beneficiary of Jesus' greatest miracle, he drops from the scene and is never mentioned again. No one asks him what it was like to be dead, or if they do he does not answer. He does not go on to be Jesus' most devoted disciple, or to preach inspiring sermons,or even to visit the sick and console the dying. Mute, he simply disappears from view.

Novelists, playwrights and poets have imagined a future for him – how, in the days after his resurrection, he sits in the darkest corner of his house in Bethany, bothered by the light, smelling of earth and incense, with twigs and grass in his hair. People kneel in front of him to ask him things, to offer him things – some bread, a bath, a skin of wine – but he does not respond. A silent, emaciated man, he is less profound than befuddled; nothing makes sense to him anymore, not his sudden death, nor his equally sudden return to life. He did not ask for either of them, and what everyone so far has either been too polite or too afraid to mention is that after all this – after all the days of pain and fever, the days of hearing his sisters weeping somewhere in the house; after everything it took for him finally to let go of his life and surrender to death – after all this, he has been hauled back into the light and *must do it all again*. He is a walking miracle; he has been brought back to life, but it is a temporary reprieve. Sooner or later he will be carried back into his tomb, and this time for good.

We must all, finally, die. As fervently as we pray for healing and long life, as glad as we are on the occasions when those prayers are granted, we must all finally die, and it is the darkest mystery each of us must face. Like Martha and Mary, we appeal to some power that will protect us from it; like Jesus we weep with the enormity of our sadness and anger at it; like Lazarus, we find no words that can make sense of it. And oh, is there anything in the world we would like better than to make sense of it all? To know why we die when and how we do, to know where death fits in the divine economy of things, to have reliable evidence that death is just a dark door into a brighter world where *everything* makes sense? If there is one word our hearts can be counted on to cry out when we are afraid, it is "Why?" *Why me, why this, why now?* As if understanding would make our fear go away. As if we were given a very good reason, like, "You are needed somewhere else," or "There is nothing more for you to learn here," then we would not be afraid? Ha!

It is not explanations we want, not for themselves; it is the security, the control those explanations might give us. Tell us why, God, and maybe we can offer a convincing argument why not. Tell us why and maybe we can be so outraged by the answer that we decide to reject it and manufacture answers of our own. Tell us anything we can handle, tinker with, control, but do not ask us just to believe – believe what? *That everything will be all right*. Like how, exactly? *Just all right*. Will I still be me? *It will be all right*. Please, God, give us something we can work with, something we can hold on to. Do not ask us to step out into the air without a net.

It is the ancient, ancient cry of the human heart: *Why me, why this, why now?* Don't you care that we perish? Give us something to hold on to – My God, my God, why have you forsaken us? They are strong words, strong questions to ask the ruler of the universe, but they are the truth of how we feel when we cannot make sense of what happens to us, when we are not given a reason. We feel abandoned, forsaken, but because the patriarchs and prophets, because Jesus himself has joined us in these words, and in these feelings, they are not something we must hide. To have faith in God, to have faith that we are in good hands, to have faith that, whether or not we understand it, the universe makes sense – that is the hardest choice any of us must ever make, and to decide that it is all true *is* to step out into the air without a net, because we have no proof, no evidence, nothing but the adamant witness of our own hearts that it is so. We simply give up the illusion that we are in control of our lives and step out. Which is why, perhaps, it is called a *leap* of faith.

I was talking earlier this week with a friend of mine about this sermon, about death and the damnation of not knowing what will happen to us. He has lost several dear friends in recent summers – men his age, mostly, who have died in a number of bizarre ways: one from a cerebral hemorrhage on his way home from a lecture tour, one from a heart attack while jogging and one, inexplicably, from a sudden lightning bolt while fishing with his family. My friend worries, of course, that he will be next, and while he worries he keeps remembering a scene from his boyhood in a southern town, how he used to traipse down to the river with some of the older boys and watch them swing far out over the fast-moving water on a rope tied to the branch of a tree. He sat and watched them arc across the sky and then let go of the rope, falling down the air and disappearing into the current. A little ways downstream their heads broke the surface and they swam back to shore, egging him on, urging him to take a turn in the air.

He was afraid, but decided to try; they were his friends, after all, and he had watched them do it. So he decided to do it too. He grasped the rope, got a running start, and swung far out over the water. At the height of his ride he willed his hands to let go of the rope but they would not – it was so far, the water was so fast, he was so afraid. He had watched how the other boys did it, but he had not a clue what allowed them to let go of the rope. So he hung there, dangling between sky and the river, until someone hauled him back to earth.

I do not know how many tries it took him before he finally let go, but he said that when he finally did, it was because of his friends. "They had all gone ahead of me," he said. "I had watched each of them let go and finally I just made up my mind that if they could do it I could to it too – without knowing what would happen, without knowing whether I would make it or how it would be – I just opened my hands and let go, because I wanted to join those who had gone ahead of me." He remembers that episode, he says, because that is what it is like now, watching his friends die. Still afraid of letting go, he has watched each of them do it and believes more and more that maybe, just maybe, when it is his turn he can do it too, if only because they have gone ahead of him.

Fine, you may say, that is a very nice story, but there is one very important difference: those boys swam back to shore to tell him everything would be all right. Who has come back across the river of death to tell us the same thing? It all depends on whom you believe, and if you believe. There was Ezekiel's miracle in the valley of dry bones for one thing, and there was Lazarus for another, although as far as we can tell he never said anything at all. And then there was Lazarus' friend Jesus, who faced his own death with great uncertainty and fear but who was willing to let go, to step out into the air without a net. Some said they saw him later and that he talked about peace, about how it had turned out there was nothing to fear after all, and that the water was fine. It all depends on whom we believe, and if we believe. It all depends on whether, when it is our turn, we can let go of the rope, let go of our illusions of control, let go of our fears and step out into whatever God-given, death-defying mystery comes next.

SCRIPTURAL INDEX

III. THE INHABITANTS OF EARTH

DOUBT
Are You the One?

Third Sunday of Advent, Year A
Isaiah 35.1-10
James 5.7-10
Matthew 11.2-11

SERVICE
Local Miracles
Proper 11, Year B
Isaiah 57.14-21
Ephesians 2.11-22
Mark 6.30-44

PRAYER
After Words
Proper 12, Year A
I Kings 3.5-12
Romans 8.26-34
Matthew 13.31-33, 44-49a

FAITH
The Automatic Earth
Proper 6, Year B
Ezekiel 31.1-6, 10-14
II Corinthians 5.1-10
Mark 4.26-34

DEATH
Without a Net
Fifth Sunday of Lent, Year A
Ezekiel 37.1-14
Romans 6.16-23
John 11.1-44